P9-B2

Coaching Writers

Editors and Reporters Working Together

ROY PETER CLARK

Dean of the Faculty
The Poynter Institute for Media Studies

DON FRY

Associate
The Poynter Institute for Media Studies

ST. MARTIN'S PRESS, New Y

Editor: Cathy Pusateri
Project management: Gene Crofts
Text design: Gene Crofts
Cover Design: Judy Forster
Cover art: Linda Draper

For information write:
St. Martin's Press, Inc.
175 Fifth Avenue
New York, NY 10010

Cloth ISBN: 0-312-06842-5
Paper ISBN: 0-312-04937-4

Library of Congress Cataloging-in-Publication Data
Clark, Roy Peter.
    Coaching writers / Roy Peter Clark, Don Fry.
        p.   cm.
    Includes bibliographical references and index.
    ISBN 0-312-04937-4
    1. Journalism—Editing. 2. Journalism—Authorship. 3. Newspaper
editors. 4. Reporters and reporting. I. Fry, Don. II. Title.
PN4778.C594   1991
808′.06607—dc20   91-61444

Acknowledgments

Excerpts by Donald Murray from *How I Wrote the Story,* ed. by Christopher Scanlan. 1986 *Providence Journal.* Reprinted by permission of the author.

Stories from the *St. Petersburg Times.* Reprinted by permission of the *St. Petersburg Times.*

Excerpts from the *Courier-Journal* by Mervin Aubespin. Reprinted with permission of the author and the *Courier-Journal.*

Excerpts from article about working with Joel Rawson at the *Providence Journal* by Bruce DeSilva. Reprinted with permission of *Rhode Island Monthly.*

From *Max Perkins, Editor of Genius* by A. Scott Berg. Copyright © 1978 by A. Scott Berg. Reprinted by permission of the publisher, Dutton, an imprint of New America Library, a division of Penguin Books USA Inc.

"Babe Ruth Bows Out," photo by Nat Fein. Reprinted with permission of Nat Fein.

PREFACE

All writers need support. The best editors know that. These editors have developed secret ways to help their reporters write with speed, clarity and power. This book teaches those secrets.

The best editors "coach" their writers, that is, they talk with them while they report and write. Good talk. They also "coach" their writers by discussing problems with them and helping solve those problems.

The best editors have evolved specific techniques for freeing and inspiring their writers. Journalists rarely discuss or analyze these techniques, but this book reveals them.

Consider this book an apprenticeship in the craft of coaching. Beginning editors and reporters need to learn these techniques together to build the newsrooms of the future, places where good work gets encouraged, recognized and rewarded.

Every journalism teacher should include coaching in every course in reporting and editing, because the secret techniques of coaching will become the norm in newsrooms by the end of this century.

To help move the profession in that direction, this book shares with students and professionals the advice and wisdom collected from the most experienced and skillful coaches in American journalism. This book summarizes decades of practical experience in newsroom coaching and converts it into handy lists of tools and techniques. Dozens of real-life examples and case studies bring the craft of coaching to life. Practical workshops at the end of chapters invite readers to practice new techniques so they can feel comfortable while coaching writers.

Until now, little academic or professional training has been available to teach aspiring editors how to support the work of writers. This book seeks to fill the void. Toward that goal, we try to practice what we preach: to build on what works and to explore solutions for what needs work; to celebrate the collaborative efforts of reporters and editors; to be open and honest about the glories and struggles of journalism; and, most of all, to be practical in a field of study where journalists need lots of practice.

No writers need more coaching than those who seek to write well about coaching. So we thank the many journalists, colleagues and teachers who have coached us while we developed our ideas on the human side of editing, and who indeed have coached us as we wrote this book. We appreciate all the help we got, and the just plain friendliness the subject seems to attract.

Acknowledgments

First, we thank our colleagues at The Poynter Institute, who keep exploring our ideas and applying coaching concepts to their own areas: management, broadcast, graphics and ethics. Of course, we've learned a lot from them too. Our colleague in writing, Karen Brown, keeps challenging us with her wit and common sense, and Valerie Hyman contributed her lively chapter on broadcast coaching. We thank Billie Keirstead and Pegie Stark, whose design sense has helped us imagine the structure and feel of this book.

The Institute staff keeps the place humming while we run around thinking and talking and teaching and coaching. We absolutely depend on our wonderful secretary, Bobbi Alsina, a real trouper and problem solver. Jo Cates, our former chief librarian, kept our in-baskets overflowing with useful clippings, and compiled the bibliography for the book. And our director, Bob Haiman, conducts the Poynter orchestra with intelligence, grace and style.

The Institute owns the St. Petersburg Times, which we regard as our laboratory for trying out new ideas and techniques. We would like to thank the staff of the paper for all they have taught us, and for their willingness to serve as our experimental subjects, so to speak. We have learned coaching techniques from friends such as Bill Adair, Tom French, Jeff Good, Jeff Klinkenberg and Mary Jo Melone. We tested our notions on dozens of editors, some of whom became in turn our teachers, especially Mike Foley and Neville Green.

The Poynter Institute serves as a crossroads for journalists, and we feel privileged to know so many dedicated and talented editors and reporters who have passed through here. We have learned much of what we know from such friends as Merv Aubespin, Bill Blundell, Foster Davis, Paula Ellis, Jack Hart, David Hawpe, Mary Jo Meisner, Mike Pride, Paula La-Rocque, Joel Rawson, Chip Scanlan and Rick Zahler. All coaches owe a special debt to Lucille deView and Paul Salsini, who have spread coaching ideas far and wide through their Coaches' Corner.

A number of teachers have helped us immensely, most especially Donald Murray, professor emeritus at the University of New Hampshire and a columnist at the Boston Globe. Murray remains the coach of all coaches, and his great ideas pervade this book. We have profited from the friendship and advice of Carole Rich at Kansas, of Ann Schierhorn at Kent State, and of Carl Sessions Stepp at Maryland. The Washington Journalism

Review, also based at Maryland, deserves special credit for publishing our early pieces on coaching, despite the fact that those articles did not fit their normal format and style.

One sad note: as we finished this book, Rene Fortin of Providence College died. We recognize him here as one who exemplified the spirit of coaching: to free the spirit of the writer. As medievalists by training and at heart, we must also thank our two oldest and wisest mentors, Geoffrey Chaucer and the Venerable Bede.

We thank the following people who acted as reviewers for the manuscript:

Linda Levin, University of Rhode Island
Raleigh C. Mann, University of North Carolina, Chapel Hill
Mike Pride, The Concord Monitor
Don Ranly, University of Missouri
Carole Rich, University of Kansas
Michael Smith, University of Maryland
Carl Stepp, University of Maryland

We thank our editor at St. Martin's, Cathy Pusateri, who prodded a misshapen mess of a typescript into whatever coherence this book has by her wise questions and insightful suggestions. We thank the team of editors and designers who helped bring the book to life, including Emily Berleth, Gene Crofts, Denise Quirk and Darby Downey. Among their accomplishments, they helped us adhere to AP style.

We dedicate this book to our wives, Karen Clark and Joan Fry, to thank them for kneading us into shape and tolerating our writerly quirks.

Finally, we wish to thank each other for 20 years of friendship and collaboration and coaching and laughter.

If any reader finds anything wrong with this book, we're not surprised, because no piece of writing ever gets truly finished. We regard it and coaching as work in progress, and we welcome all suggestions and ideas.

Roy Peter Clark and Don Fry
St. Petersburg, Florida

CONTENTS

11 A Vocabulary for Coaching   101

Writers and editors need a shared vocabulary for talking about their craft. A list of basic terms will help them see their work in a new way and talk about it more effectively.

WORKSHOP 109

12 Coaching for Revision   110

In this case study, some simple questions and observations lead to powerful revisions in a story.

SUMMARY 117

13 Coaching in Broadcast   118

Coaching techniques work effectively in broadcast newsrooms. A veteran reporter describes how to get started.

SUMMARY 121

PART FOUR   WORKING TOGETHER

14 A Climate for Coaching   124

Editors must create an environment in which good work is encouraged, recognized and rewarded.

A Great Experiment in Newswriting 130   SUMMARY 135

15 Talking to Each Other   136

Journalists can learn from the story of a young reporter who suffered in a newsroom where he received little guidance and feedback. Where there is no coaching, reporters often struggle and fail.

SUMMARY 141   WORKSHOP 142

16 How to Get Coached   143

The writer is a full partner in the coaching process. The smart and tactful writer can get the most out of an editor.

Coaching Your Editor 148   SUMMARY 152   WORKSHOP 152

HOW TO USE THIS BOOK

You're reading the first book ever published on coaching writers, which differs from all books ever written on writing and editing. So, here's some advice on how to read it.

First, our audience: you. If you're a reporter, assigning editor, copy editor, journalism educator, undergraduate or graduate journalism student, or just someone interested in coaching, this book speaks to you. We have addressed it to professional and student journalists at the same time. We hope that college students who discover this book will keep it and refer to it throughout their careers as journalists.

You will hear us talking about "your newsroom," apparently assuming you work in a newsroom. We talk about "coaching your reporters," as if you're an editor, and "getting your editor to start coaching," as if you're a reporter. At times, we address you as if you're a copy editor. We assume that professionals tend to play several of these roles, maybe all, in a career. As a reporter, you can learn how to think like a coaching editor, and someday you may become one. Even if you don't, you'll be able to understand editors better.

We believe that professionals can imaginatively think like other players in their newsrooms, and that such empathy will help all those players.

But suppose you're a student, without a newsroom. We assume that any student reading this book will likely become a professional someday, so we're treating you like a professional right now and throughout this book. Learn to think and imagine like a professional, and you'll be one. And besides, you can work for the student newspaper and have your own newsroom. Today.

Second, we have included workshops that ask you, professional or student, to assume certain roles. Some workshops will seem more appropriate to your status than others. You can just do the ones that fit you as you are now, or better, you can do any workshops that seem likely to help you learn new viewpoints and techniques. Or you can do all of them. Use the workshops in any way that helps you.

Third, we include all sorts of lists of techniques and ideas. We want to spread them to help people accomplish great journalism. So, feel free to make copies of those lists and post them for other people to read. Please indicate where you got them, so other people can find this book.

Fourth, for purposes of explanation, we have assumed a general model of newsroom organization that may not match yours. So, we'll explain our model and let you make the appropriate adjustments.

In this general model, editors assign stories to reporters or approve reporters' story ideas. Then the reporters collect information and write their stories, which they submit to desk editors. Those editors edit the stories and pass them on to copy editors for finish and layout. Broadcast stations have reporters who work closely with photographers and report variously to news directors, assignment editors or show producers.

As you will soon discover, we wrote this book to reform the way journalists act and the ways they treat one another and their readers. We celebrate those journalists who undertake their work with an almost missionary fervor. And we hope this book will help create newsrooms alive with a sense of vision and democratic purpose.

So, don't be surprised if, on occasion, we criticize or even satirize conventional ways of thinking or working that survive in your newsroom and in your head. Our goal is not to offend, but to inspire change. That begins with you. As you read this book, don't be afraid to reflect upon your own behavior as a journalist. If you want to change yourself, this book suggests some maps for the journey. Remember, we're all in this profession together.

Finally, coaching is a young art, and we're inventing it day by day by doing it. If you figure out some different or better ways to do some of the things we discuss here, let us know. Just call the Poynter Institute in St. Petersburg, Florida. Our number is (813) 821-9494. Ask to talk with Roy Clark or Don Fry. We're ready to listen.

INTRODUCTION

Coaching writers is the human side of editing. Coaching involves nothing more than talking with writers, in certain ways. A city editor can help a reporter plan a story. A copy editor can help a colleague write a headline. A reporter can respond to the story of a friend.

Even people with junior status can coach. A copy clerk can coach the ace columnist. A student can coach a teacher. All you need are some basic reporting skills: Can you ask good questions? Can you get people talking? Can you listen? Can you observe and see patterns? Can you read with curiosity? Do you like stories? If you answered "yes" to these questions, you can coach. If you also have a sympathetic nature, so much the better.

When some journalists hear such talk, they get nervous. Discussion of the human side of editing offends their sensibilities. Reporters should be tough and independent. Say "nurture" and they hear "nursemaid."

"I thought editing had no human side," quipped one editor with a laugh. He should know.

Tradition tells us that editors grumble, yell, slam phones, wad stories into balls, chew cigars and chew out writers, especially young ones. A cartoon in a 1941 book titled "Nose for News: The Way of Life of a Reporter" tells the story. It shows a fat city editor sitting on the back of a young reporter, pounding on his head with both fists. The caption reads: "The new reporter will be called on the carpet a few times by the boss. In this picture, though, it would seem that the reporter has made more than a slight mistake."

Writers hate editors who butcher prose, suppress creativity and turn exciting experiments into tired formulas. Editors hate writers who indulge themselves and forget the needs of readers. Traditionally, both groups would rather bitch and moan than consult and collaborate. Coaching can change that.

Although coaching is a new concept, it is an old practice in American newsrooms. Many distinguished journalists look back with fondness on some early editor who taught them the craft. The form of instruction was not always the most enlightened. The stories that reporters tell sound like boot camp, with every editor a drill sergeant.

Jon Franklin, twice a Pulitzer winner at the (Baltimore) Evening Sun, recounts the tale of his own mentor, an editor named G. Vern Blasdell, who whipped young Franklin into shape:

> Eventually he'd pull himself together, look at me sternly, and point his finger at the straight chair he kept beside his desk. I'd slink over to it and sit, bottom on the edge of the chair, while he proceeded to rip my copy to shreds. When he was done with me, I'd crawl back to my typewriter and do it over again, and again, and again, until he pronounced it readable. Thus I learned to write without inspiration or ego, relying solely upon knowledge, and in the process became a professional. . . . Five years at the mercy of Vern left me with an ulcer, a discipline, a craft, and a love for the old man that was equal to what I once felt for my father.

Writers young and old crave such critical attention, although they could do without the ulcer. They want editors to discuss story ideas, to show them new ways of seeing and reporting, to help focus and organize stories, to discover new approaches to storytelling, and to help them identify what works and what needs work. In other words, they want to grow in their craft. This growth can be accomplished without animosity, in ways that build a relationship of trust between writer and editor.

Until his retirement in 1989, editor Sheldon Binn set the standard at the New York Times. His supportive style of editing and enthusiasm for well-crafted stories inspired a generation of reporters, including Francis X. Clines:

> He was on the city desk for all my years in the city, and he was just a very smart, very gentle, very curious man. You would report to him at the end of the day, and that really focused what we were doing every day. You had to tell him a story. . . . By the time you wrote the story, you were reinforced in what was amusing or important. He was always human.

It surprises some journalists that each activity could be called "coaching." Tom Romano, an expert writing teacher, says, "The most brutish, insensitive people I have ever known were coaches." He imagines some barrel-chested goon making him run up and down stadium steps, screaming "Use active verbs!" or "Show, don't tell!" in his face.

In its origins, the word has an academic rather than athletic meaning. In the middle of the 19th century, British university students coined the word *coach* to describe the tutors who helped them with their studies outside class.

The word was adapted by Donald Murray in 1978 as a newsroom teacher at the Boston Globe. The name *coach* was needed to describe a new creature in American journalism, a writing teacher who would work in the newsroom as an outsider, tutoring writers and creating an environment in which good work was encouraged, recognized and rewarded.

The writing coach filled a vacuum left by editors. While the coach developed reporting and writing talent, the editors set the news agenda, attended meetings, made sure the computer system was working, checked vacation schedules and attended more meetings. More and more they seemed to abdicate their teaching responsibilities. They didn't even yell and chew cigars anymore. They just wore nicer and nicer suits.

We are left with a generation of editors who think they don't know how to coach, who are afraid to coach, who don't want to coach, or who don't think they have time to coach.

There are many exceptions, of course, men and women who understand the human side of editing and its importance in producing great work in American newspapers. These editors embrace traditional values but stay open to new ideas. They encourage strong reporting as well as good writing. They carve the time to coach out of their busy schedules. They see working with writers as their first responsibility, not the last thing they get around to.

Until now, editors who wanted to learn to coach had few places to turn. Most books on editing ignore the human side of the process. You can learn copy editing skills or design concepts or the production process from books. You can learn how to word-edit a story from anonymous examples, but every editor knows that it takes one skill to improve a piece of writing and another to improve a writer.

Most editing books work on the assumption that any editor can change any story in any way, and that reporters can improve their work by reading the changes in the paper the next day, intuiting the concepts behind them and applying them in the next story. Missing from this scenario is one human being talking to another.

Editors are not chosen for their human skills. Too often, they are selected because they were good writers, or because they were bad writers. Being a good writer helps, but it is not enough. A good writer may lack the skills and disposition to support the work of other writers. Few newspapers have developed apprenticeships to allow new editors to learn from the best veterans.

This book will teach you how to coach. If you are the new assistant city editor, read it and become a hero in your newsroom. If you are the editor of a college paper, learn how to help the freshman reporters. If you are a good colleague, learn how to help your friends. If you want to improve as a writer, learn how to attract the kind of feedback you need. If you are the top editor at a newspaper, learn how to make your writers and editors happier and more productive. If you're a copy editor, learn how to communicate better with the rest of the newsroom. If you're a teacher, learn how to teach writing individually, perhaps teaching students how to coach.

Part One, The Art of Coaching, defines coaching and teaches the basic strategies of collaborative editing. Here you will learn dozens of new techniques. You will also learn the important distinction between "coaching writers" and "fixing stories," and how both skills contribute to teaching the craft.

Part Two, The Human Side of Editing, describes the work of the best writers and editors, models for those who wish to excel. Reporters and editors can learn the craft from one another, united by a devotion to readers and a shared sense of mission.

Part Three, Coaching the Writing Process, ties the act of editing to the writing craft. Here you can study the most important parts of the writing process, learning how to pass along techniques. You can begin to build a critical vocabulary for discussing writing and editing with reporters.

Part Four, Working Together, offers ideas on how you can reach a point where coaching is commonplace. This section explains how to create an environment in newsrooms in which coaching is possible.

"Coaching Writers" encourages editors to embrace the strategies and values of coaching. We want this book to improve your career and along the way, change your life. The craft of coaching is easy to learn. But to become the editor or writer you want to be may require something of a conversion, a new way of seeing, a change of heart. A book can only point the way. Only something deep within the head and heart offers the courage to change.

PART ONE

The Art of Coaching

CHAPTER 1

The City Editor Coaches the New Reporter

The date was June 14, 1978. Roy Clark had begun a new career as a general assignment reporter at the St. Petersburg Times. He had already received two assignments and carried them out with vigor and courage. The first was a piece on the new telephone book, the second a daring report on daylight-saving time. But on this day, Clark sat at his desk in the newsroom, dreaming of great investigative stories, of exposés, of Pulitzers. His city editor, Mike Foley, approached him.

"Okay, Killer, we just heard over the police radio that a car has fallen on a man. Get out there, and don't come back without a story."

The cub reporter sped out to the accident and took notes for an hour, talking to witnesses, family members and paramedics. After finding out that the man would be treated and released from the hospital, Clark returned to the office a bit disappointed.

"What'd you get, Killer?"

"Well, Mike, a car did fall on a man, but he's okay. It's not much of a story."

"How the heck does a car fall on a man?"

"Well, he was kind of a big guy. He had his head up under the car working on his brakes. The jack slipped, and the frame pinned his head to the driveway."

"How did they get it off him?"

"Oh, some teenage boy was walking along the street, and he heard this guy scream. He jumped over a fence and ran past a guard dog and helped lift the car off the guy."

The reporter saw his editor's pupils dilating.

"You said this guy was big. What do you mean big?" asked Foley.

"His wife said he weighed over 350 pounds."

"How did they get him to the hospital?"

"They had to call four extra paramedics to lift him into the ambulance."

As he heard himself answer his editor's questions, the reporter realized he had a story. He learned a lot that day, especially that he had a lot to learn about news judgment.

About an hour later, the reporter finished the first draft of his story, with this lead: "A 135-pound teenager helped lift a 2,000-pound car off a 378-pound man Wednesday."

Foley said: "You may have too many numbers in the lead. Don't be afraid to tell it like a story. It'll be very short, so don't feel you have to cram everything into the top. Could you start it with the kid hearing the scream?"

A half-hour later, the reporter returned with a new draft:

> Carey Graham was walking home Wednesday morning when he heard a scream.
>
> Seconds later, he was helping lift a 2,000-pound car off a 378-pound man.
>
> Graham, a 16-year-old student at Lakewood High School, was walking home after working in his grandmother's yard when he heard the yells of 55-year-old Robert Gasper behind Gasper's house at 955 22nd Avenue S.
>
> "I took a shortcut home through the alley when I saw them working on the car," said young Graham. "I heard someone say, 'Ow! Help! Get this damn thing off me!' I knew that the car must have fallen on him."
>
> Graham ran into the yard and found Gasper's son-in-law, 27-year-old John Cross, straining to lift the frame of the orange 1969 Mazda off the head of Gasper.
>
> "I didn't think about anything but lifting that car," said Graham. "It didn't feel heavy. I didn't even know until later that I had cut my hand." When the car budged, Gasper was able to roll out from under.
>
> Gasper had been trying to replace the front right brake shoe when a scissors jack slipped. Gasper's head was pinned between the car frame and the concrete driveway.

An emergency fire rescue unit arrived and gave first aid to Gasper. Paramedics called for reinforcements before moving the 378-pound Gasper onto a stretcher.

"It took six men to pick him up," said paramedic Matt Larbalestrier. "He lacerated his ear. And you could see the mark on his skin where the car fell on him. It must be a hell of a feeling to have a car on your head."

Gasper was taken to the emergency room of Bayfront Medical Center where he was treated and released.

Thanks to his editor, the cub reporter wrote a story that got good play in the paper the next day and was read word for word on a radio news program. Foley's response to the reporter reveals many of the basic strategies of coaching.

Coaching does not have to take much time. It probably takes two minutes for the editor to give the reporter the assignment. It takes less than a minute of debriefing for Foley to convince Clark he has a story worth telling. It probably takes another minute for Foley to help the reporter rewrite the lead and find a good way to organize the story. Total coaching time: less than four minutes.

Coaching can happen at different stages of the process. Foley does not just give the reporter an assignment and correct the mistakes in his final draft. Instead, he intervenes after the reporting, when the reporter is struggling to find a lead. This work at the front end of the process saves valuable time for Foley. He won't have to spend precious minutes repairing a broken story on deadline.

The coach asks the reporter good questions and listens to the responses. In doing so, he draws upon Clark's experience at the scene, milking him for details that may or may not be in the reporter's notebook. Even though Foley has years of experience, and Clark very little, the editor still treats the reporter as the expert on this story. Clark does not know what he knows, but Foley's questions draw the story out of him.

The coach is not afraid to tell the reporter what he thinks. The tone of Foley's questions and observations is supportive and collaborative. He has made himself a partner in the effort to improve the story. He tells the reporter that his first lead may have too many numbers in it, but the editor doesn't stop there. He suggests an alternative: beginning the story with the rescuer hearing the scream.

The coach communicates his values. Through his questions and observations, the editor lets the writer know what he thinks is important. Information is important. Specific details are important. Telling a good story is important. The reader is important. The process begins building a relationship between reporter and editor. The reporter will hear his editor's questions echoing in his head on the next story. Debriefing and conferring will become more efficient.

The editor coaches the writer not just on long features but also on breaking news. Too often, coaching is associated with special projects, extraordinary features and creative writing. Foley coaches his reporters on breaking news stories. They are the meat and potatoes for the reader, and the good editor wants them written and reported with energy and enthusiasm. Every story, every headline, every digest item deserves the writer's care and the editor's attention.

Practicing the human side of editing requires no exotic strategies. Most editors have already tried the basic techniques: quick conferences, asking good questions, preparing and debriefing the reporter, taking the story seriously, making good observations, offering alternative approaches, bouncing back the story to the writer and letting the writer know, now and over time, what you think is most important.

SUMMARY

- Coaching does not take much time and may save time.
- Coaching can take place at different stages of the writing process.
- The coach asks good questions and listens.
- The coach is not afraid to tell the reporter what he or she thinks.
- The coach communicates values.
- The editor coaches the writer, not just on long features, but also on breaking news.

WORKSHOP

1. Make a list of all the words that come to mind when you think of the word *coach*. Now make another list for the word *editor*. Discuss what the lists have in common and how they differ.
2. In the introduction, an editor is quoted as saying, "I thought editing had no human side." Play the role of amateur psychologist. What realities lie behind that joke?
3. Interview a few journalists, asking them: "Who taught you to be a good journalist? Tell me what that person was like, and how he or she was

helpful." What are the common themes in their testimony? Are you surprised by anything?

4. Some readers prefer Clark's first lead ("A 135-pound teenager helped
   lift a 2,000-pound car off a 378-pound man Wednesday") to the revision
   ("Carey Graham was walking home Wednesday morning when he heard
   a scream.") Conduct a debate in which you argue which lead is more
   effective. With the help of a friend, play the roles of writer and editor
   and discuss both beginnings.

5. Make believe you are Clark's editor and that you are seeing his story for
   the first time. You can help him improve the story in any way you
   choose. What questions would you ask him?

6. You are the police reporter. Over time, your editor approaches you with
   these brief snippets of news, which she has heard on the police radio:

   a. A car has fallen on a man.
   b. During a drug bust, a man stabbed a cop with a hypodermic
      needle.
   c. A heavyset, possibly pregnant, woman has robbed a convenience
      store.
   d. There is a fire in an abandoned warehouse near public housing.
   e. After a Little League baseball game, a parent threatened an
      umpire.

   With a friend, conduct a brief conversation on what you might find when
   you go out to the scene. Give yourself only two minutes on each case.

7. Read Clark's story again. What works in the story? What needs more work?

CHAPTER 2

Sharing Control of the Story

Mike Foley might have been tempted to wrest control of the story from his inexperienced reporter. Instead, he moved his writer toward a new way of telling the story, but allowed him to undertake the revisions. This restraint and coaxing built the confidence of the writer and taught him to use an important new tool: the narrative lead.

Editors who do not work this way waste time fixing broken stories. The lead is in the fourth paragraph. The story is six paragraphs too long for the allotted space. A crucial piece of information is missing, but the reporter is nowhere to be found. So, without consultation, the editor reworks the lead, cuts the last six paragraphs and writes around the hole in the story. The editor must work quickly, because several other stories await repair. Even if the writer is available for consultation, some editors choose to seize control, taking over the process of revision and making the story theirs.

Who should control the story? The easy answer is "the editor." As Gene Roberts, former editor of the Philadelphia Inquirer, said: "A paper ought to be a participatory democracy until 20 minutes before deadline; then it

becomes an absolute monarchy." All journalists face the tyranny of deadline and the control it exercises.

Almost every journalist knows at least one case in which reporter and
editor settled their disagreements about a story with physical violence. At
one paper, a young reporter, checking on final corrections in copy, was
pushed out of the composing room by the editor.

More common are scenes of reporters and editors shouting into one
anothers' faces or of acts of violence against property: slammed doors,
kicked desks, overturned wastebaskets and ripped-out telephones. Don
Fry saw an editorial writer lose a shouting match with his editor and then,
as he stalked away, "accidentally" catch her computer monitor with his
elbow and knock it on the floor.

Less dramatic, but more symbolic, are the many cases in which frus-
trations over a story have led to this confrontation:

Reporter: "I give up. Have it your way. But take my name off the story."
Editor: "Your name isn't on it yet."

All stories need some degree of editorial touch-up and repair, but the
good editor prefers to leave control with the writer, even if significant
changes are needed. The editor does so because the reporter knows the
story, and stealing control can lead to inaccuracies and distortions. Helping a writer fix the story allows the writer to grow in the craft and feel fully
responsible for changes in the copy.

Every editor must learn to fix stories, but fixing is not the same as
coaching. Coaching is the human side of editing, fixing the literary side.
In other words, the editor coaches the writer but fixes the story. Editors
must understand all the implications of this crucial distinction.

Editing serves the reader by making the story and the writer better at
the same time. Editors accomplish both by helping the writer fix the story,
rather than by repairing it themselves.

In some newsrooms, an editor may collaborate closely with a writer on
a story, working through the process to develop a satisfying draft they both
can be proud of. They may then lose control of the story, turning it over
to production editors licensed to fix the story in any way they see fit.
Without reform of such a system, reporter and editor lose confidence in
their ability to get their best work in the paper.

Bill Blundell of the Wall Street Journal sees coaching as "front-end
work" and believes that his paper, famous for its bank of talented rewrite
editors, should spend more time earlier in the process to help reporters
shape stories that will not require extensive revision. If necessary, the editor can confer with the writer at the idea stage, before or after the report-

ing, when the writer is looking for a focus, after a draft has been written, right up to publication. But fixing, by definition, occurs near deadline.

Fixing has an important short-term benefit: getting the story up to the standard at which it can appear in the paper. Coaching feels better and lasts longer. A conversation between an editor and a reporter today will help the reporter next month or next year. The editor seeks to establish a relationship with the writer that will help both of them grow in their crafts over time.

Coaching builds confidence, while crude fixing undercuts the confidence of the reporter. Most editors can remember their worst reporting days, those mornings when they picked up the newspaper and read a story quite different from the one they handed in the night before. When fixing is the only mode of editing, the writers rarely feel they are growing in the craft. Often, the writer does not agree that the fixer's changes made the story better. Perhaps no one has explained the changes so the writer has a chance to learn.

Fixing may turn writers and editors into adversaries, whereas coaching unites them as partners. Some radicals believe that writers and editors should be "equals," but most journalists think that "partners" is good enough. If the story succeeds or fails, writer and editor should share the credit or the blame.

Yet the process often resembles civil war. The writers think the editors are butchers who hack their copy to death. The editors think of their writers as prima donnas who resist guidance and direction. Fixing may breed contempt. Coaching creates collaboration.

Collaboration need not mean dependency, because coaching fosters independence in writers. Coaching is not a crutch or a pacifier. When coaching works, the confidence of writers grows with their knowledge of the craft and their understanding of the editor's values. Fixing forces reporters to depend upon the editor, because writers give up when they hand in story after story and find them, without consultation, radically altered.

To build the confidence of the writer, the coaching editor uses sincere praise as a tool. To improve a story, the editor helps the writer identify what works in a story. Then the pair can concentrate on what needs work. For example, the reporter may have used a strong quote to illustrate a point but placed the quote in a position of weak emphasis. The editor can respond, "This quote really gets at what the mayor thinks about the new stadium proposal. What would happen if we moved it up under the lead?"

On the other hand, the fixer, strapped for time, purges the story of its imperfections to get it into the paper the next day. Perhaps the fixer resembles too much your worst English teacher, the one who highlighted your every mistake in red ink, scrawling helpful comments like "AWK!" in

Watch Your Language

An experienced reporter from New England tells the story of a humiliating conversation she had with an editor. Unhappy with one of her stories, he called her into his office. "You must have had your head up your ass when you wrote this one," he told her. The reporter gets angry every time she thinks of it. "I still have to work with him on occasion," she confesses, "but I do everything in my power to avoid having him work on one of my stories." The issue here is not only language, but also dignity and respect.

Since the 1960s, profanity by men, women and even children has become more acceptable in our society. In our own times, films, rock songs and other media have bombarded us with language that continues to test the limits of our tolerance.

The newsroom, like the traditional locker room or barracks, has been a breeding place for offensive language, coarse and creative. Shocking language has its uses in art, journalism and ordinary human discourse. Because it can be used as a weapon to hurt or control another human being, abusive profanity should be eliminated from any formal conversations between writers and editors.

We anticipate this complaint: "But what happened to old-fashioned, straightforward honesty? What if the story sucks? Isn't it a part of our duty to communicate this to the writer?" But a story never "sucks." There are appropriate and professional responses: "This story has so many mechanical errors in it that we just can't get it in the paper. Proofreading is part of your responsibility." "You need to do a lot more reporting to prove that assertion. Who else can you talk with?" or "This is unacceptable work. You've done so much better in the past. Is there something troubling you that I should know about?" Even "You're fired" is better than the potential degradation that is a product of abusive profanity.

The traditional newsroom environment is changing. The stereotype of the swearing, cigar-chewing city editor is vanishing. That character cared about journalism and perhaps inspired others through fear. But those days are over. The new editor also maintains high standards but treats reporters with dignity and respect. The new editor also cares about the effects of language and never uses it as a weapon against others.

the margins. The coach looks for strong words and specific achievements as well as problems needing solutions.

To be effective, the coach inspires experimentation and risk-taking. The best writers take chances in their writing. Francis X. Clines of the New York Times says that he wants to take enough risks that he occasionally fails in print. Donald Murray laments that he rarely sees interesting failures in the newspaper. The best editors respect traditional journalistic values but want to help writers "push the outside of the envelope" to discover new ways of defining news and telling stories. The worst editors force their writers to see the world through tired formulas. Working on deadline, they tend to be suspicious of innovation and experimentation and to enforce conventional approaches to stories.

Finally, the coaching editor asks questions and listens, while the impatient fixer tells the writer what to do: "Well, look. Your lead is in the 14th paragraph. Move it up, and maybe we can get this thing in the paper."

Coaching and fixing are not mutually exclusive. They interlock. The abuses of fixing are dangerous only when fixing occurs in the absence of coaching. In fact, fixing a story can be one of the coach's most important tools.

Neville Green was Roy Clark's editor on a story written about Clark's father. Green liked the story very much and planned to publish it, but he was concerned that the piece was too sentimental and unfocused. "Give me a chance to show you how I would make it better," Green told the writer, assuring him that his comments were suggestions, not final editions. Green suggested several changes, including deleting a number of paragraphs to sharpen the focus, and rewriting the ending to defuse the sentimentality. The writer agreed to all the changes. Not only did Green improve the story, but he gave the reporter some new tools for his workbench.

Green probably spent 10 minutes or so going over the story with Clark, a luxury they could afford for a non-deadline story. The question remains: Even if they have the ability, do editors have time to coach? People who quickly answer "no" have surrendered to the pressures of daily journalism.

Perhaps there is another way. Perhaps a minute of coaching at the idea stage and two minutes of coaching after the reporting can save the editor five precious minutes on deadline. Editors who coach testify that this is true. Add it up: three minutes of coaching saves five minutes of fixing.

This kind of coaching on the fly is called "process coaching" or "short coaching," as opposed to "retrospective coaching," in which the editor and reporter sit down at length away from deadline pressure to talk about the writer's strengths and weaknesses.

The editor knows that coaching time is well spent, even if some fixing is necessary. This process creates confidence and craft. The reporters come to believe in the ability of the editor to help them and in their own ability to learn new techniques and new ways of seeing that will enrich the reader's experience.

SUMMARY

The editor coaches the writer.

The editor coaches throughout the process.

Coaching develops the writer.

Coaching builds confidence.

Coaching builds on strengths.

Coaching unites writer and editor.

Coaching fosters independence.

The coaching editor inspires risk-taking.

The coaching editor questions and listens.

The coaching editor shares control.

The editor fixes the story.

The editor fixes on deadline.

Fixing gets the story in the paper.

Fixing undercuts the writer.

Fixing identifies weaknesses.

Fixing divides them.

Fixing creates resentment.

The fixer leans on conventions.

The fixer directs.

The fixer takes control.

WORKSHOP

1. Discuss at length who should control a story, the reporter or the editor.
2. Some newspapers call themselves "writers' papers"; others are known as "editors' papers." What do you think people mean when they use such descriptions?
3. Think of some editors you know and about how they work. Are they primarily coaches or fixers? Explain this distinction to them, and ask them how they see themselves.
4. Every newsroom has stories about loud arguments, sometimes violent ones, between reporters and editors. Why do you think such things happen? Have you ever experienced such an argument? Can you imagine a way in which a disagreement over a story could have been resolved through more peaceful means?

5. Have you ever been angry about how someone senior to you responded to one of your stories? Write a paragraph on the case, explaining why you felt the way you did.

6. Has anyone ever been angry with you for how you responded to a story? Put yourself in that person's shoes and defend his or her point of view.

7. Make separate lists answering Donald Murray's four questions:
   a. How can an editor help a writer?
   b. How can an editor hurt a writer?
   c. How can a writer help an editor?
   d. How can a writer hurt an editor?

   Share your lists and discuss them.

CHAPTER 3

How to Consult with Reporters

Writers at newspapers large and small all crave *feedback*. The word hurts the ears, like the electronic squeals of heavy metal music. People who like feedback march to the beat of a different eardrum.

When writers say they want feedback, what do they mean? They want an editor to listen to what they have to say about a story. They want praise. When they write a good story, they want editors to recognize and reward their efforts.

They want specific advice and criticism. "Nice story" is better than nothing, but what really helps is "I thought the anecdote about the schoolgirl helped you focus the story," or "I think you ended the story one paragraph too late. You didn't need that final quote."

They want editors to serve as test readers, to respond to work as readers rather than as bosses. They want editors who can show them new ways of seeing, thinking and writing. To grow, they need the help of "teaching pros" who can offer a better organization for a story, a way to uncover a key piece of information or a strategy for rewording a sentence.

They want all significant changes made to their stories explained. They want, whenever possible, to make those additions or revisions themselves. They want brief encounters with helpful editors at key points in the process: when the idea is germinating, when the reporter returns from collecting information and after the draft comes in.

These encounters are sometimes called "conferences," and they reflect a style of work that Donald Murray has termed "consultive editing." In a book titled "How I Wrote the Story," Murray describes the primary aims of this type of editing:

1. To make use of the knowledge and experience of the writer.
2. To give the writer primary responsibility for the story.
3. To provide an environment in which the writer can do the best possible job.
4. To train the writer, so that editing will become unnecessary.

Every editor should have a toolbag filled with strategies on how to confer with writers. These can be practiced until perfected. Eventually, these methods become second nature for both writers and editors and build relationships of trust and collaboration.

Busy editors must work quickly, because they have no choice, but some conversations between writers and reporters take an hour or more. Perhaps a major series is being reported, or an editor wants to evaluate a reporter's first six months of work. With careful planning, editors and reporters can find time in a work day for such extended discussions. But long conferences should be rare.

More often, the editor has to work in 30-second to five-minute bursts, offering feedback and advice spontaneously, when the writer needs it. The reporter returns from covering an important meeting, and the editor milks the writer for information: "What happened? What will readers want to know? How much space will you need? When can I have it?"

Maybe the writer will write a lead and want to try it out before proceeding. The editor may suggest an alternative approach, or just hand it back to the writer with a nod of approval. Even a grunt or a smile can be a conference.

Journalists who practice conference techniques at the Poynter Institute are often amazed how much they can accomplish in only two minutes. In that interval, a writer can communicate important information to the editor. Both writer and editor can learn something from that conversation.

In most conferences, the writer should speak first, with the editor listening carefully to what the writer has to say. The editor may initiate a conference with "How can I help you?" or "How's it going?" but only to open the writer up. No matter how much experience the editor has, she has not experienced the news event. The writer is the expert on that day's trial testimony or the speech at the business luncheon. But the writer may not know what he knows, and can benefit from hearing himself talk about the story. The editor learns from listening and can then suggest new sources of information or fresh approaches to writing the story.

In effective conferences, the writer does most of the talking. And the editor who hears good things out of the mouth of the reporter can make sure that those things get in the story. A veteran editor once told a story about a reporter who went out on a Coast Guard ship to cover the rescue of two men lost at sea. The reporter heard the men's account of their ordeal: how they were adrift for days, and how sharks had circled their rubber raft, even brushing the bottom of the raft with their dorsal fins. The editor, hearing the tale, looked forward to receiving a great adventure story, but when he began to read, he was disappointed. Finally he yelled: "Where are the sharks?!" The editor has to make sure the story in the paper is as good as the one out of the reporter's mouth.

When reporters talk, good editors must listen. Only a confident editor can be open and patient enough to hear the writer out, to accept an emphasis that contradicts an editor's presupposition on how the story should turn out. Editors who listen show their receptivity to writers in their body language and their facial expressions. Writers looking for feedback are sensitive to the most subtle signals. They've seen editors' eyes glaze over or stare into space. The editor who leans forward and looks the writer in the eye is prepared to receive and respond.

It helps for editors to discern how the writer feels about the work so far. During a coaching workshop at the Poynter Institute, reporter Christopher Scanlan wrote a sample lead that a roomful of teachers and editors began to hack apart. "It sucks," yelled a voice from the back of the room. After several minutes of this badgering, Scanlan asked an important question: "Why didn't anyone ask me how I felt about the lead?"

Why, indeed? Just because a writer hands in a story does not mean that the writer is satisfied with it. Often the writer hands in flawed work. The writer may know why the work is flawed. An editor's few simple questions will help the writer to reveal these flaws to the editor: "Tell me about the story." "What should I be looking for?" "How do you feel about this piece so far?"

The response from the writer may be, "I like the way the lead turned out, but I'm not sure about the ending," or "I know it's too long, but I can't find a place to cut it." Such responses are valuable for the editor. If the editor agrees with the criticism, she is saved from having to deliver bad news to the writer. If she disagrees, at least she can take the writer's notions into account.

Given the nature of writing and writers, this dynamic can get tricky. The writer may hand in the story and say something like "This is really stupid." But what does he mean? He may mean "I really think this is a stupid story, and I want you to know that I know it's stupid," "I don't really think this is stupid, but I want to hear it from you," or "I'm not sure if this is stupid or not, but in case it is, I want you to hear it from my lips." No one said that working with writers would be easy.

Coaching editors help writers identify the most important problem that needs to be solved. In classrooms and in newsrooms, the traditional process of writing and teaching works this way: the writer gets an assignment at the beginning, hands in the story without consultation, and has all his mistakes corrected for him. There is a better way.

Conversation between reporter and editor leads to a shared vision of the key problems in the story. The reporter travels to the state prison to conduct an interview with a death-row inmate scheduled to die the next morning in the electric chair. At the last minute, the interview is called off. Reporter and editor are disappointed. What should the reporter do next? What new shape will the story take without the interview? Conversation will help them find some new angles for reporting and writing.

Without such conversation, the editor is too often surprised and frustrated by the appearance at deadline of stories with terrible flaws. The lead is buried, important information is scattered incoherently through the story and many sentences just don't work. With other stories awaiting her attention, the editor spends five minutes on quick repair, moving a low paragraph up to the top, jury-rigging a transition here or there, and chopping out the worst sentences. "At least," says the editor to herself, "we got it in the paper."

A better way is to diagnose the key problems in the story at various points in the process before the story comes in. A lack of focus produces a bad lead, which makes incoherence inevitable, infecting the very diction of the story. An editor who consults with a writer on the focus of the story will find the time well spent. She won't have to prune all those moribund sentences on deadline.

The editor's best questions are those that help the writer to discover what needs to be done next. At any point in the process, the writer can hit a wall. A key piece of information is missing. A source won't go on the record. The writer can't think of a lead, or writes one that leads nowhere. The right questions, even simple ones, can help the writer over the hump.

One day, Don Fry was wandering around a newsroom when he saw a writer sitting in obvious agony at his computer terminal.

"Need help?" asked Fry.

"For the life of me, I can't write a lead on this story," said the reporter.

"What's the story about?"

"It's hopeless. It's about how the Arts Council just gave a medal to the best accordion player in the state."

"Sounds interesting to me."

"It isn't. I don't have anything. It's hopeless."

"Do you have any good quotes?"

"No. The guy could barely speak English."

"Did he say anything funny?"

"Well, as a matter of fact, he said that Lawrence Welk has ruined accordion playing in America because people think you can't play anything on an accordion but 'Lady of Spain.'"

Fry smiled at the writer. The writer smiled at Fry and typed a lead inspired by that quotation.

Writers often, out of frustration or laziness, try to sneak weak stories past busy editors. Unable to explain the complexities of a bond issue, the reporter tries to cloud his misunderstanding with foggy prose. The vigilant editor will find the problem and, thinking of the readers' needs, will call him on it. This process of turning a flawed story back to the writer for repair is called "bouncing back." Editor as brick wall.

But the technique can be beneficial for both writer and editor. It saves the editor time on deadline, and it instills confidence in the writer who knows that, even when the story needs work, the editor trusts the writer to undertake it.

Cynthia Gorney, a prize-winning writer for the Washington Post, puts it this way:

> I know there's a whole school of thought in newspapers that experienced, professional reporters just do it and don't need their hands held. I think that's crap. What makes an editor great is support. I don't know a writer who isn't insecure. An editor has to say: "We think you're wonderful. We know you can do wonderful work, even when your work is terrible."
>
> Usually I know that a story is flawed. I just send it in anyway, because I'm confident that they're going to help me figure out what's wrong with it. A great editor will make you feel like a real trouper, a truly talented person for being able to fix a story, for being able to send something in that's flawed and then make it better.

Donald Murray suggests these methods for consulting with writers at different stages in the life of the story:

> When the assignment is given: Ask the writer to suggest ways of reporting and writing the story. If your idea turns out to be the writer's idea, then you're ahead of the game. If the writer's idea is better, you're way ahead. If it isn't, then you have your chance to speak.
>
> During the reporting: Be available to the writer so the writer can solve the writer's own problems by talking them through. Use your own experience as a resource. Let the writer use you as a test reader.

Before the first draft: Listen to the writer tell you the focus of the story, the approach, and the length. Give the writer room, if possible, but if you have a strong problem with the focus or the approach, talk it out. Set a deadline and a length. Listen to arguments against either, but then make a final decision and stick to it.

At delivery of the draft: Encourage the writer to tell you what works best and what problems may exist before you read the draft. Your job is not to judge the writing, but to collaborate on the production of an effective story. You need the writer's knowledge to help you read the story intelligently.

After the reading of the draft: Confirm or modify or flatly disagree with the writer's evaluation of the work. If editing or revision is necessary, invite the writer to suggest how it will be done, and let the writer do it, if possible.

After publication: Get the writer to tell you the history of a particularly good story, or invite the writer to discuss how a story that didn't work could be written and edited more effectively in the future. It's best to build on strength, though. Don't look for the weakest aspect, but the strongest. It's more helpful to reinforce what works, rather than what does not.

As a good editor, you must prove to the writer that no evil consequences will flow from sharing work with you. By the time you get to work with a writer, that writer already has a personal history of success and failure in writing and in working with teachers and editors. In many newsrooms, well-intentioned editors find reporters suspicious of editors and resistant to coaching. Edna Buchanan, the famous police reporter for the Miami Herald, says she follows three simple rules: "Never trust an editor. Never trust an editor. Never trust an editor."

The way to earn the trust of writers is to demonstrate that conferences work. For example, a reporter who goes to an editor with an idea needs to emerge from the conference with the sense that she's had a fair hearing. All writers look for editors with open minds and good hearts.

Too often, the experience of the reporter turns her off to the idea of consultation. One editor turns down almost all ideas. Another never talks to a writer except to convey negative criticism. Another wastes time and leaves stories sitting on her desk. Another looks off into space when a reporter is speaking. Another loses his temper easily and cannot engage in useful conversation without turning it into argument.

Reporters learn something important from these experiences: how to avoid being edited.

We've all had this experience: we look around the room and see someone approaching our desk. How do we feel about this person? Are we happy to see him or her? Do we look forward to some consultation? Or does this person's appearance spell trouble, so that we retreat into our bunkers? If you are an assistant city editor, for example, you want your reporters to look forward to a productive conference when they see you coming. You want to build a positive history with a reporter, even if that person has had poor relationships with editors in the past.

It helps to be somewhat predictable and to ask the most important questions over and over again. Tom Stites, a features syndicate executive who got his start at the Kansas City Star, learned his craft from an exacting city editor, Ray Lyle. In editing a story, Lyle would ask his reporters the same question, "What happened?" until it burned into their psyches. When you came back from the reporting, Lyle would ask, "What happened?" When you were struggling with a draft, Lyle would ask, "What happened?" That single question helped a generation of Star reporters to clarify thinking and sharpen prose. Reporters in the field had to start thinking about what happened because they'd have to face Lyle's tough question when they returned to the office.

Even questions that seem more about form than content can help the writer. "How long do you think it will be?" forces the writer to evaluate the material in the notebook. "When can we have it?" demands a response that involves judgments of all kinds, not only "How fast can I write?" but also "How much time and energy does the story merit?"

The editor's questions become echoes in the writer's head. They create models of journalistic thinking that not only shape a particular story but also resonate for years and influence careers.

What does the reader need to know?
How can you make this clear?
What's the story about?
Have you found a focus?
What's your best quote?
Who are the most interesting people in your story?
Have you thought of an ending?
How do you know that?
What did it look like?
What happened?

These questions, asked again and again, become lenses through which reporters see the world.

Conferences can be verbal or non-verbal, as short as 10 seconds or as long as 10 minutes. They can be conducted in the office, in the hallway, at lunch, over the phone or sitting side by side at a terminal.

An editor who uses all of these methods makes consultation a normal and regular part of workday conversation. It helps for the editor to get out of the chair and away from the computer terminal. The enlightened editor does not call reporters to the editing area with a bullhorn. On occasion, the editor will venture into the reporter's territory to talk about stories.

These brief encounters help both writer and editor, preparing them for the next step in the process. A simple "How's it going?" from the editor may evoke useful information from the writer: "Well, I've got my lead, but I'm not sure where I'm going after that."

In brief conferences, body language is especially important. Is the editor really interested in the reporter's problem? Does the editor *look* interested? Or, as the reporter speaks, is the editor's gaze flashing around the room in anticipation of the next useless stop? Does the editor shout over the reporter's shoulder to another person, "Hey, you, don't go away. I need to talk to you." And then, "Now Joe, what were you saying?"

Body language cannot be conveyed over the telephone, but long distance conferences have their own special style. A good editor lets the reporter speak, listens, asks good questions, and treats the caller like a colleague, not an unknown telephone solicitor. "You've been out on the road for two weeks," complains a sportswriter, "and you call into the office after a night game, looking for a little friendly chatter, and all you get on the other end is this robot with the same routine: 'How long is it? When will we get it? We'll call if we have any questions.'"

Editors may need the same kind of telephone training received by suicide hotline counselors!

Finally, editors should not be afraid to coach without reading the story. Something funny happens to many editors when a writer hands in a story. "I can't help myself," says one. "When someone shows me a story, I want to start making it mine."

To resist the urge to fix a writer's copy, try coaching without looking at the text. Leaving the piece in the writer's hands allows that writer to maintain control of it while it's in progress. The right questions help the writer decide what to do next and save the editor valuable time:

"How's it going?"

"I've finished a quick draft. Wanna see it?"

"Let's talk first. How do you feel about it so far?"

"I'm happy with everything except the quotes."

"What's wrong with them."

"Well, Judge Brockton got real long-winded and confusing on why he threw out the verdict. He just rambled and used a lot of legal jargon. He spoke in these run-on sentences, which I think will confuse the reader and make the story sort of boring."

"Why not just paraphrase him?"

Editing Side by Side

Veteran writing coach Donald Murray believes in editing side by side.
He says:

One of the most effective conference variations is the editing conference, in which writer and editor sit side by side at the video tube. The
editor may make the changes in the text on the screen, or may suggest
changes orally, but in either case the attitude is the same, "I'd like to play
around with this. I don't know whether I can make it work better, but let
me try to show you what's on my mind."
   When I do this as a writing coach, I have several simple rules:

- The text belongs to the writer. I'm not back on my old job of rewrite.
- All writing is experimental. We don't know what works until we try
  it. Failure is normal and instructive. From failures, we see ways to
  achieve success.
- Fooling around with language is fun. We are playing a game of
  voice and meaning, and we can't afford to take it too seriously.
- I rarely make one suggestion. I point out several alternatives,
  usually three. This might be the lead or that or something back
  there. I wonder what would happen if this were cut or made longer
  or tightened up. I keep revealing the possibilities of the text, so that
  the person I'm working with will learn to see and take advantage
  of those possibilities.

"I'll try, but I'm worried about getting it wrong."
   "It sounds to me as if you're not perfectly clear in your own mind about
what's going on. I think you need to call him again. If he won't give it to
you straight, see if you can get it from the public defender or the DA, and don't
be afraid to say 'Judge, I'm having a hard time trying to make this clear to
my editor. Can you give it to me in language that even he'll understand?'"
   "I'll try it."

   All these strategies may provide more feedback than any writer could
stand, but too much feedback is much better than none. A number of
things happen to an inexperienced writer who gets no feedback, all bad
from the editor's point of view. The writer leaves for a paper that gives feed-

back. The writer becomes a pain in the neck, complaining about the short-comings of the editor and spreading seeds of discontent. The writer comes to enjoy neglect, resists editing and falls into dangerous habits.

So, the next time a writer demands feedback, as an editor you have two choices: hand the writer an album from the rock group Megadeth, or listen to what the writer has to say and try to figure out what he or she is looking for.

SUMMARY

- Work quickly.
- Let the writer speak first.
- Listen to the writer.
- Figure out how the writer feels about the work.
- Help the writer to identify the most important problem.
- Ask questions to discover what needs to be done next.
- Work throughout the process.
- Turn responsibility for revision back to the writer.
- Allow no evil consequences from conferring.
- Be predictable and dependable.
- Use a variety of consulting strategies.
- On occasion, coach without reading the story.

WORKSHOP

1. Think of all the meanings of the word *feedback*. What kind of feedback do you need to become better in your work? What kind of feedback do you give others? Interview some friends or colleagues to see the kinds of feedback they need. Do you see any patterns?
2. Seek permission to watch a conversation between a writer and an editor about a story. Be a quiet and careful observer. Take lots of notes, and pay attention to the subtleties of body language and word choice. Write a brief statement describing the encounter.
3. Coach a writer on a story, experimenting with at least one of the techniques described in this chapter. Record this session on audio-tape or, if possible, on videotape. Review the tape on your own, and critique your performance. If you had another chance, what would you do differently?

4. Interview some editors to determine how many writing "conferences" they conduct each day. Now interview some writers on how often their editors consult with them about their stories. Do writers and editors agree?

5. Most conversations about stories occur at the assignment stage and after a draft of the story is handed in. Is this true in your experience? Are you the kind of person who benefits from consultation throughout the process? Discuss your preferences with others.

6. Which of the consulting strategies described here have you used before? Are any of them completely new to you? Add any of your favorite strategies that have not been discussed.

7. Find a friend with whom you can discuss the craft of editing. Have a conversation in which you exchange your favorite coaching strategies and weigh their strengths and weaknesses.

8. In a small group, look at a draft of a story with the writer present. Each person gets to ask the writer one question, which the writer must answer in one minute. Ask the writer which question he or she found most helpful.

9. Do the same exercise with another story and another writer. This time each person gets two minutes to coach the writer. Ask the writer which coaching session he or she found most helpful.

10. Conduct some practice coaching sessions in which you speak as little as possible. Focus, as powerfully as you can, on listening to what the writer says about the story.

11. Try one coaching session without speaking at all, using only body language.

PART TWO

The Human Side of Editing

CHAPTER 4

Good Editors Study Good Writers

Stuart Dim tells this story about his experience as a young reporter at Newsday:

Almost 30 years ago, I learned a great reporting lesson from the late Al Marlens, my managing editor at Newsday. He taught me about detail.

I was covering a gangster's trial. I took pains to describe his gray sharkskin suit, his white-on-white shirt, his blue silk tie, his stickpin, his pinky ring. I was proud of the word picture I had painted, and I turned in my story.

About three hours later, about midnight, Al came over and said, "Stu, not a bad story, but what about the handkerchief?"

Handkerchief? Al told me he wondered whether the gangster also wore a handkerchief in his breast pocket. "Gee, Al, I don't think he wore a handkerchief."

Al told me to call and ask him. Call a gangster at midnight to ask about his handkerchief! He had to be kidding. He wasn't. So I called.

The gangster answered the telephone. I did some sweet, fast talking. Incredibly, the gangster agreed to walk to his closet and look at his suit jacket.

"Yeah," he said, he had a handkerchief in his pocket.

"What color?"

"White."

"How many points?"

"Five."

I went back to my typewriter and inserted the handkerchief information. Al Marlens stopped by my desk again and said, "Stu, now that's reporting."

Al Marlens recognized in Stuart Dim a reporter with a nose for a story, an eye for detail and an ear for language. In conferring with Dim, Marlens used a variety of coaching techniques. He asked the writer questions about the story, testing his memory and his vision. He recognized in the writer something promising, a desire to paint a word picture, and built on that strength. Finally, he refused to settle for merely good work. He pushed the writer to a new level of specificity, a new level of excellence, a new level of expectation for himself.

Good editors watch good writers. They study their habits and idiosyncrasies, like a trainer preparing a boxer for a big fight. They learn writing tricks, reporting strategies, ways of thinking and seeing, news values and templates. By understanding how to support the good habits of strong writers, editors learn how to teach these habits to weaker ones.

We can match every characteristic of a "good writer" with techniques a supportive editor might use to get the best out of that writer.

First and foremost, good writers see the world as a storehouse of story ideas. If they can get out of the office, they can find a story. They can't walk down the street, drive to the mall or watch television without finding something, and probably 10 things, to write about.

Good editors tap into this reservoir of curiosity. They ask questions too. They join in the quest for good story ideas. They keep themselves open and supportive, especially at the beginning of the process.

Good writers prefer to discover and develop their own story ideas. They have an eye for the offbeat and may find conventional assignments tedious. They appreciate collaboration with good editors and devise strategies for avoiding bad editors and what they perceive as useless assignments.

Editors can act as collaborators and partners in the quest to produce good work. Good editors stay out of the way of excellence and innovation. They allow writers to turn story assignments into their own ideas, often by brainstorming with them.

Good writers collect information voraciously, which usually means that they take notes like crazy. They are more concerned with the quality of information than with flourishes of style. They prefer to describe themselves as "reporters" rather than as "writers." They regard the title "reporter" as a badge of honor.

Good editors stay on the same wavelengths as their writers. They develop an eye for the concrete and specific detail that only good reporting produces.

Good writers tend to spend an inordinate amount of time and energy on their leads. They see the lead as the most important part of the story, the passage that invites the reader into the piece, signals the news, and teaches the reader what to expect. They tell war stories of rewriting a lead a dozen times until they "got it right."

The best editors recognize the time and energy good writers invest in leads. Writers treat leads with greater respect than other parts of the story. Thus, editors recognize that writers may not devote the same kind of critical attention to other parts of their pieces, so they help writers improve the middles and endings.

Good writers immerse themselves completely in the story. They live it, breathe it and dream it. They plan and rehearse the story all day long, writing it in their heads, weighing their options, talking it over with editors, always looking for new directions and fresh information.

Writers immersed in stories often lose their objectivity and detachment. Because they know too much, they can lose control of the material. They can no longer role-play the reader or select information intelligently. Good editors gallop in to their rescue.

Many good writers "bleed" rather than "speed." In the words of the great New York Times sportswriter Red Smith, they "open a vein" when they write. Because their standards are so high, their early drafts seem painful and inadequate. But when a deadline looms, or a big story breaks, adrenalin kicks them into a different gear. They can speed when they have to.

Slow writers tend to hand their stories in late, driving the desk crazy. A vindictive editor can create unpleasant consequences for deadline destroyers, such as holding a story for a day. But good editors obtain printouts of early drafts from slow writers, so they can get a strong sense of the story and prepare to move quickly at the deadline crunch. They give a lot of slack to slow writers who produce great work.

The best reporters devote a lot of time to the mechanical drudgery of organizing the material, what Associated Press reporter Saul Pett describes as "donkey work." They make a fetish of creating careful filing systems. They develop idiosyncrasies that help them build momentum during the writing process: pilgrimages to the restroom, chain-smoking, pacing, daydreaming, junk food orgies, or self-flagellation.

The good editors learn writers' idiosyncrasies and use them to advantage. They can read body language to recognize when to confer or when to leave a writer alone. They offer coffee, cokes, smokes, junk food, lemon cough drops, whatever it takes as inducements and rewards.

Good writers rewrite their rewrites. They love computer terminals because they permit maximum playfulness during revision. Good writers move paragraphs around, invert word order for emphasis, find stronger verbs and occasionally kill the entire story for a fresh start. Unfortunately, they are rarely satisfied with their final stories and, burdened with imperfection, can hardly bring themselves to read their own work in the newspaper. Ego drives writing, making the writer suffer and, at times, insufferable.

Let's face it, even good writers can behave like jerks. But writing anxiety is real, and good editors respect it. They confer on changes to let a writer participate in the process of making the story better. And sometimes, they make a writer hand over the story and just go home.

In judging their work, good writers tend to trust their ears and their feelings more than their eyes. Some stare at the screen with their lips moving, praying that the inner music will reach their fingers. While editors "look for holes in the story," writers want to "make it sing."

Good editors do not edit with their eyes alone. They tune in to the sounds and rhythms of the prose. When they make a change, they test the effect of that change on the sound of the story, usually by reading the passage aloud. They check to see if the transitions still work.

Good storytellers love to tell stories. They constantly search for the human side of the news, for voices that enliven the writing. Their language reflects their interest in storytelling. Rather than worry about the five *W*'s, they regale their colleagues with anecdotes, scenes and narrative bits. They tend to answer even the most theoretical questions with war stories, jokes and parables.

Good editors tap into the values of the best writers and ask good questions to elicit stronger anecdotes, better quotations, concrete details and interesting human characters. Good editors have their own fund of war stories to help reporters remember heroic efforts and the best work produced at the paper.

Thoughtful writers write primarily to please themselves and to meet their own exacting standards, but they also see writing as a transaction between writer and reader. Unlike many other journalists, these writers have confidence that readers will appreciate sophisticated work. They treasure readers and want to reward and protect and inform them. They speak possessively of "my readers." They take responsibility for what readers learn and understand in a story.

Good editors strive to help writers by representing readers. They spot story elements that seem self-indulgent rather than directed toward the needs and interests of readers. They defend their suggested changes in terms of readers.

The best writers take chances. They love surprising and unconventional approaches to stories. They don't mind failing in print occasionally because those failures test their inventiveness. They appreciate editors who tolerate experimentation, but who will save them from falling on their faces. They secretly wish to produce the best, most original piece in the newspaper every day.

Reliable editors provide a safety net for their writers. The writer wants to test the boundaries, so the good editor is open to risk-taking by the writer but is also honest. Good editors have no reluctance to tell the writer what works and what flops.

Good writers read voraciously all their lives, mostly novels, and they like movies. They collect story ideas and forms from other genres. They love words, names and lists.

Good editors also tend to read avidly. They share their reading interests with writers and other editors. They talk about movies with colleagues. When they debrief their writers, they always ask for the name of the dog, the color of the car, and the brand of the beer. They praise writers for the skillful use of interesting words in a story.

Good writers tend to write too long, and they know it. Good editors work hard to convince reporters that shorter is better, because it usually is, but they never cut stories arbitrarily. They agree on length in advance and remain flexible. They help the writer to select the best information and to prune the weaker elements.

Unlike other journalists, who may stop caring for the reader after they finish polishing the lead, the best writers, like Stuart Dim, use transitions and the promise of strong endings to keep their readers cruising along. They drop rewards along the way to keep readers on the path. They write such good endings that the copy desk has no temptation to cut from the bottom.

Good writers want their readers to read every word. The best editors, like the late Al Marlens, want that too.

SUMMARY

- Good writers see the world in story form.
- Good writers prefer their own story ideas.
- Good writers collect information voraciously.
- Good writers spend time on their leads.
- Good writers immerse themselves in the story.
- Many good writers are bleeders rather than speeders.

- The best writers invest time in organizing materials.
- Good writers rewrite their rewrites.
- Good writers trust their ears and feelings more than their eyes.
- Good writers love to tell stories.
- Good writers remember the reader.
- The best writers take chances.
- Good writers devour novels and movies.
- Good writers write too long, and they know it.
- The best writers guide the reader all the way to the bottom of the story.

WORKSHOP

1. Pick out a magazine or newspaper story that you really like, by a writer you do not know. Make a list of the things that you like about it, trying to be as specific as possible.
2. Based on your reading of this story, write a page imagining what the writer is like, as a person and as a journalist. Try to contact the writer. Share with the writer your affection for the story. Ask the writer questions about how the story was written.
3. Make a list of the things you think you do best as a writer. Share these with a friend.
4. Compare your behavior as a writer with the traits listed in the chapter. What positive and negative traits do you have that are not listed?
5. Who is the best writer you know? Describe that person's values and work habits. If possible, interview that person to confirm your impressions.
6. Young writers sometimes find it difficult to fill up an assigned writing space. As they mature, they sometimes tend to write longer stories than the material justifies. Describe this tendency in your own work. Do people think your stories are too long? What do you think?

CHAPTER 5

Models for Editors

Name the writers you admire. Now name their editors.

Most journalists know more about writers than they do about editors because writers work up front, editors in the background. Writers get bylines, editors anonymity. Writers talk and write about their craft; editors may not know how.

Journalists need more testimony about how good editors work, on both the literary and human sides of the craft. How do editors make writing better, and more important, how do they make writers better? We might take what looks like a detour and begin a search for this wisdom with America's most inspirational book editor: Maxwell Evarts Perkins.

In more than 30 years as an editor for Charles Scribner's Sons, Perkins became friend and mentor to some of the greatest American writers of the century: F. Scott Fitzgerald, Ernest Hemingway, Ring Lardner, Marjorie Kinnan Rawlings, James Jones and, most difficult of all, Thomas Wolfe.

Helping Fitzgerald improve "The Great Gatsby" may seem different from helping a cub reporter with a police brief. But many of Perkins' admirable qualities would help any newspaper editor. Far more than any editor in our history, Perkins understood the marriage of the human and literary sides of editing. A number of newspaper editors follow the Perkins style of supportive editing today, reflecting some of his most important values and methods in their own newsrooms.

Respecting Individuality

First, good editors respect the individuality of the writer. Perkins once said:

> Don't ever get to feeling important about yourself, because an editor at most releases energy. He creates nothing. A writer's best work comes entirely from himself. . . . In the end an editor can get only as much out of an author as the author has in him.

Vince Doria, former executive editor of The National, has used this golden rule to nurture some of the most talented writers in American journalism. When Doria headed the Boston Globe sports department, he had the tough job of finding a replacement for star baseball writer Peter Gammons, who switched to Sports Illustrated. He wisely resisted the temptation to find "another Gammons." Instead, he picked Dan Shaughnessy. "No matter what Dan did," says Doria, "he wasn't going to be Peter Gammons. Dan's his own man. He may have been tougher on the beat than Peter, more objective. I've tried to praise him for his strengths."

Doria thinks like Perkins:

> I've always looked at each writer as an individual. When you do that, though, you've got to make sure you're not being perceived as unfair. If I have a terrific writer who is good at long features, I may give him twice as long to produce. I know he'll need the time, and will use it. You need to let people understand that writers work at different paces and at different levels of productivity.

Encouraging Idiosyncrasies

The good editor understands and tolerates the idiosyncrasies of writers. Perkins described Thomas Wolfe, who stood 6 feet 6 inches, and his work habits:

> Mr. Wolfe writes with a pencil, in a very large hand. He once said that he could write the best advertisement imaginable for the Frigidaire people since he found it exactly the right height to write on when standing and with enough space for him to handle his manuscript on the top. He writes mostly standing in that way, and frequently strides about the room when unable to find the right way of expressing himself.

The Philadelphia Story

Once one of the weakest newspapers in the United States, the Philadelphia Inquirer now ranks among its best. Credit for the change
usually goes to former editor Gene Roberts, who joined the paper in
1973 to instill a new style of writing and editing.

Along the way, he hired Maxwell Evarts Perkins King, the grand-
son and namesake of America's most celebrated editor. King was
four in 1947 when Maxwell Perkins died, but he grew up absorbing
stories about editing and, after a career as a reporter, became city
editor, associate managing editor and in 1990 succeeded Roberts
as editor.

"I saw the Inquirer transformed from a traditional newspaper
operation into a paper where editors dealt with writers as a resource
rather than a tool," says King. "The story had a life of its own, and the
editor's job was to make sure nothing screwed up two things: the
story and the writer."

The pressures of time and space make newspaper editing a
special challenge, says King, one that inspires in him a respect for
his colleagues:

What was special about Max Perkins was his ability to help a writer clear
hurdles. Steve Lovelady can do that on deadline. He can get into the middle
of a story that everyone knows is broken, find a way to fix it, and bring the
writer along with him as part of the process.

It was thrilling to be part of that change, and more thrilling as an editor
than as a writer, more of a feeling of breaking new ground. As a writer, you
felt privileged to be part of a process that allowed you to do your very best
work. As an editor, you felt part of a process of fundamental change in
newspapering. That was really exciting.

Perhaps Perkins came to tolerate eccentricity in writers because he was
eccentric himself. He talked to himself on commuter trains and was
famous for wearing hats indoors.

Frank Barrows, an idiosyncratic editor at the Charlotte Observer,
agrees with Perkins that editors should not only tolerate eccentricity but
celebrate it. In 1969, Barrows used to arrive at the Observer with a grocery
bag filled with bottles of Tab. "I'd camp out at my desk for periods as long
as 48 hours. To enforce my concentration, I would lash myself to the chair

with a big black belt I had found. It would keep me from getting up and wandering around." Sometimes he'd wear a pair of airport noise blockers on his ears.

Barrows' clothes matched his headgear: "I had two shirts, a brown polo shirt and a green polo shirt, and I'd wear them on alternate days." His editors would say, "He's weird, and he only has two shirts," but nobody ever tried to change him because his stuff was so good.

"Today I'm the deputy managing editor," Barrows says. "I wear a white shirt every day. It's possible that I only have *one* shirt. That leads me to believe that the 'white shirts' in the newsroom should not get too hung up on the eccentricities of writers and reporters."

Passing Out Praise

Good editors use sincere praise to bolster the confidence of their writers. Wolfe wrote to Perkins: "Your words of praise have filled me with hope, and are worth more than their weight in diamonds to me." Scott Fitzgerald enclosed this note to Perkins with the manuscript of "The Great Gatsby": "Naturally I won't get a night's sleep until I hear from you, but do tell me the absolute truth, your first impression of the book, & tell me anything that bothers you in it." Temporarily ignoring some problems, Perkins sent this cable: "THINK NOVEL SPLENDID."

While he was city editor of the Louisville Times, David Hawpe, now editor of the Louisville Courier-Journal, used the newsroom as a theater to praise his writers.

> You have to know what's in the paper in enough depth so that, when you walk into the newsroom, you can spontaneously remark with some precision on the achievement of people who are sitting there. On occasion, you do it for show. I have actually run out into the newsroom with a piece of copy with one word circled, put it down on the author's desk, said "Great verb!" and then walked off. This creates an incident. This means people in the vicinity come over to see what it's all about, remark on the aberrant behavior of the editor, but pay attention to the praise that was delivered.

This supportive, even theatrical, style of editing may offend journalists who have grown up in a cooler tradition. Says Hawpe:

> The old city editor liked to define himself by the number of people he fired. Praise, when given, was supposed to be delivered in the most grudging way possible. It was a minimalist theory of praise: that if you understate it enough, you will call attention to it. For me, it's a much happier thing to do it the other way.

Values of an Editor

Paula Ellis knows that writers can get angry when you mess with their stories. One pulled a gun on her. Apparently, he didn't like the way his story had been chopped in half on deadline, so, quite drunk, he confronted Ellis with his displeasure. Fortunately for American journalism, he did not fire. Nor was he fired! But Ellis learned an important lesson: writers, even bad ones, take their stories seriously.

That was a long time ago. Now, as a top editor at The State in Columbia, S.C., she expresses strong opinions on writer-editor relationships and represents a strong model for others to follow. Here are some of the things she believes in:

Getting Ahead of the Story
This means focusing on the impact and looking at where the news is going. This develops from constant conversation with reporters. I'm having a brainstorming session on Wednesday on the U.S.-Soviet summit, which is a month from now.

Telling Stories
Everyone loves a well-told story. We should remember that as we wail about the future of the industry. Maybe stories aren't being told well enough. I read all kinds of stories, including children's books. I'm a big fan of ballet and look for the story in the dance. I figure out what the emotional center is, the natural points of tension, the threads that pull people through. Those kinds of narrative apply to news. If I read a story that I like, I go back to figure out what I liked about it, so I can apply it.

Avoiding Newsroom Stereotypes
When you come in as editor, everyone has a book on someone else that they want to share with you. There's the official one, the one the person has on himself, the one from peers and colleagues. All are points of view. I don't want to be limited to one official point of view. Editors don't spend enough time interviewing reporters on how they view themselves or where they want to go.

Sharing Control
Editors think they're appointed as seers. They believe they are in control because someone has put them in control. But as editor you have to do a lot of reporting, acknowledging that the official structure is not always the way that things get done.

Understanding Reporters

You've got to figure out what their level of play is. Part of it is talking to them about their careers. People will know their writing problems, what they feel comfortable doing, where they need to stretch. You want to have a relationship of trust where a reporter will tell you just about everything.

Specific Criticism

As editor, I read every story about three times. The first time I read as a reader. What I get at is the big holes, the big areas of confusion that I can feel. I read it again as an editor, where I diagnose the good and bad. Then I read it again and think about how I'm going to explain my feelings about the story to the writer. How to explain it is an area where editors need a lot of work and training. Every editor needs to devise a language to communicate what they want done in a story, where they feel it's falling short and where they think it's good.

You have to be as specific as you possibly can. These days it's a trick for editors to say, Well, I really like the story, but . . ., then have about fifty buts. You have to be specific about what you like and what you don't like. You need specific proposals on how you would fix what you don't like, so they don't feel beat up and helpless. And don't pretend to have an answer for a problem if you don't have one. You can say, Let's explore this together.

Getting Your Values Into the Writer's Head

About a week ago I got a letter and some clips from a student I taught in Indiana. She said, "I never write a story without knowing that you're there." Or a reporter says to me, "I knew you would ask that."

Performance Evaluations

I believe in them. It forces people who won't talk any other way to talk. Then there is the benefit of writing things down: this is what we agree to, where we want to go, what our needs are. Things become much clearer in the writing down of them.

Building Confidence in Writers

Writers are generally insecure people, worrying about everything. They also do a job where they have their noses in everybody else's business, and that creates a lot of insecure behavior. It's easy for editors to pass all the risk down to the persons on the beat. We editors need to be clear about responsibility and be willing to say more often, "I've assumed the responsibility and the risk."

Creating a Sense of Community
You've got to be in a community of writers where people have a comfort level that feels unofficial. We're going to be experimenting, talking constantly, walking around, trading things, passing paper back and forth.

Taking Risks
As far as this idea of risk-taking in newspapers, we're still just talking about it, not close to doing it. I still see very formulaic stories.

Taking Care of Yourself
There is a dark side to all supportive relationships. People will take whatever you have to give. You keep on giving and giving, and you have nothing left. That's why you focus on your good writers, so you have something fun to do.

Paula Ellis says she learned all this not at the knee of some wise editor but by watching things go wrong. "Many people have mentors from whom they have learned something important. What I've done is watch people behave inappropriately and thought: 'I'm just not going to do that'."

Unblocking Writers

Good editors help their writers conquer writer's block. Douglas Southall Freeman told Perkins that his four-volume biography of Robert E. Lee "would never have been finished but for the encouragement I received at your hands. Many a time, when composition was lagging, a word from you prodded me on."

Jack Hart, who coaches writers at The Oregonian, says that "writer's block is a failure of nerve, so the first thing you have to do is build confidence." Hart, like Perkins, works on both the human and literary sides of the equation. "If they have to ask for help, they need some encouragement," says Hart. "They've lost faith in their ability to handle the material to some degree. The next thing the writer needs is some intermediate goal. You don't shoot for the moon. You say, 'Just write me a lead and an outline, and we'll use that for discussion.'"

Hart often concentrates on organizational problems to help the writer build momentum: "If you have writer's block, it means you're lost.

You don't know what to do or where to go next. You need a map, an overview, a vantage point to see the forest, and that's what the editor can help you with."

Perkins could see possible story structures that were invisible to the writer. Hart applied the same method in a recent case: "I read the story and did an outline on a sheet of paper. As soon as she saw that outline, it was like scales falling from her eyes. She could deal with things one at a time."

Hearing Voices

Good editors get their voices into the writer's head. Alice Longworth, daughter of Theodore Roosevelt, collaborated with Perkins on her memoirs. Perkins questioned her about her memories and feelings throughout the process. According to Perkins' biographer, Scott Berg, "As she wrote, she imagined Perkins standing over her shoulder, asking her questions. Within five or six months, Mrs. Longworth's writing had improved. 'All those "Maxims" finally sank in,' she said."

Mary Jo Meisner, former city editor of the Washington Post, works hard to become the voice in the ear of the reporter. "Like Jiminy Cricket," she says.

"The only way you can do it is through trust, not through your position," she says. "If they see you stand up for their stories, treat individuals fairly, not play favorites, and take an interest in their interests, they'll start listening to you."

In a practical sense, Meisner likes to work at the front end of the process, asking good questions and giving some direction at the idea stage. "I try to visualize the story from the beginning in what I think is its most perfect state," she explains. Without being directive or manipulative, she tries to communicate that vision to the reporter, mostly through conversation and negotiation.

This style of editing is not for the faint of heart, says Meisner:

> You have to think through a story, ask hard questions about it, and work through the reporter to get them answered. Good reporters like to be challenged. You're building the story together through lots of talk. You ask a lot of questions, like you're the next-door neighbor and you're intrigued by it and want to know more.

Handing Out Books

The good editor inspires writers by sharing things to read. Author James Jones remembered Perkins as being "like an old-time druggist. Whenever he saw you getting sluggish, he prescribed a book that he thought would pep you up. They were always specially selected for your condition, perfectly matched to your particular tastes and temperament, but with enough of a kick to get you thinking in a new direction."

Steve Lovelady serves as associate executive editor of the Philadelphia Inquirer. Lovelady's appreciation for good writing comes from a life of careful reading, so he shares works of fiction and non-fiction with writers about to undertake new assignments. Like Perkins, Lovelady picks the book to match the interests and needs of the writer. The new Middle East correspondent may get "The Red Badge of Courage" or the Civil War stories of Ambrose Bierce or a passage from Richard Harding Davis, the famous World War I correspondent.

Reading may provide models for direct imitation, but more important, it subtly influences the writer's voice and style. Lovelady also hopes to "instill a certain humbleness. One thing you learn from reading is that there's nothing new under the sun, that, in the words of Willa Cather, 'There are only two or three human stories, and they go on repeating themselves as fiercely as if they had never happened before.'"

Lovelady learned these habits from his editor at the Wall Street Journal, Bill Blundell. Lovelady remembers that

> when Bill found an extraordinary piece of writing, he'd try to outline the story the way the writer might have outlined it. It told him how the person's brain worked during the creative process. He'd type stories that others had written, on the premise that if you'd type it out, you'd retrace the creative steps the writer took.
>
> When I was a cub on the Wall Street Journal, trying to figure out how to write one of those great page-one stories, I'd take the paper home at night and study a story I particularly admired to find out how the writer got from A to Z.

Revising Revisions

The good editor persuades the writer to revise, especially by cutting. Perkins once advised Wolfe: "It does not seem to me that the book is overwritten. Whatever comes out of it must come out block by block and not sentence by sentence." Berg, Perkins' biographer, points to a four-page passage about Wolfe's uncle that got reduced to six words: "Henry, the oldest, was now thirty."

Foster Davis, an editor with the Charlotte Observer, regards helping reporters to cut their stories as one of an editor's most difficult and important jobs. He recalls a case in which an Observer reporter was arguing with his editors about a long package of stories. Davis says, "I got turned to in desperation, like the U.N. peacekeeping force."

The reporter handed him a main story and five sidebars, a total of 180 inches. Davis read everything three times, his usual practice. "It was terribly overlong," says Davis. He told the reporter: "Fifty percent of the words are doing nothing for you. This sidebar and that sidebar ought to be combined. This sidebar is so obscure, it's not worth publishing at all."

In the spirit of Perkins, the process began with major surgery, excising great chunks, before the word-editing began. Davis describes the process as "a comradely, but no-beating-around-the-bush transaction."

Davis thinks that writers will always need good editors to keep them from writing too long. "If you're a good writer," he says, "you're always competing against yourself. Is this year's best going to be better than last year's best? Best is hard to measure. Column inches are not."

Getting It Out

The good editor tempers perfectionism with reality. Perkins often wanted to continue work on a manuscript but gave up the effort because he knew, in Berg's words, "that an editor too must eventually give up a book."

Neville Green, managing editor of the St. Petersburg Times, has learned how to midwife a story that grows and grows inside the womb, but just doesn't want to get born. Green worked for more than a year with writer Tom French on a narrative of a murder trial that became the longest series in the paper's history, the equivalent of a 250-page book.

Writer and editor had to reassure each other constantly. "We knew we had a really good story," said Green. "Well, with even more time, we'd have a fabulous story."

Green gave French a deadline: the stories would be in the paper by the end of the school year, before families went on vacation and the snowbirds flew north. "I set a solid target date for the story," says Green, "and held it over his head." Green understood how the deadline would send his writer into overdrive: "From March to June, he never took a day off," says Green. "Once there was a firmness about when it would appear, I knew that an enormous effort would be forthcoming."

All these newspaper editors share with Perkins the virtues of imagination and persistence, in Berg's words: "The vision to see beyond the faults of a good book, no matter how dismaying; and the tenacity to keep working, through all discouragements, toward the book's potential." Replace *book* with *story*, and you have advice that any newspaper editor could embrace.

Perkins was a man of letters who loved editing, a person who could "strive for anonymity" and find satisfaction in helping others. An admirer once asked Perkins why, given his obvious literary talents, he did not write himself. "Because I'm an editor," he said.

SUMMARY

- A model editor respects the writer's individuality.
- A model editor understands and tolerates the writer's idiosyncrasies.
- A model editor uses sincere praise to bolster the writer's confidence.
- A model editor helps the writer to conquer writer's block.
- A model editor gets his or her voice inside the writer's head.
- A model editor inspires the writer by sharing things to read.
- A model editor persuades the writer to revise, especially through cutting.
- A model editor tempers perfectionism with reality.

WORKSHOP

1. Debate this premise: "Every editor should write at least six stories per year for his or her publication." How could a busy editor create the time for writing? What would be the effect on the staff? On the editor?
2. Read the collection of Max Perkins' letters, "From Editor to Author." Write a brief character sketch of Perkins based on the voice and personality that come from the letters. List three things that made him a good editor.
3. If someone like Perkins suddenly became your city editor, how would you feel? Would anything worry you?
4. Ask reporters to name their best editor. Does one name keep coming up? Describe the character and working habits of this special editor.
5. Make believe you are Perkins. Pick out a story, and share it with a friend or colleague. Match the story to your sense of the needs of the writer. Talk about the story with the writer.
6. Is it necessary for editors to suppress their own egos and work in the background? How then do editors have fun and gain job satisfaction? Is there such a thing as a typical "editing personality," or is that a myth?

CHAPTER 6

Coaching for Confidence

All leadership styles, including heartless tyranny, work some of the time, but no single style will benefit every follower. Understanding the needs of different kinds of writers enables editors to adjust their styles to get the most out of each kind. The writer who is willing and able to do a job needs little more than a "Go get 'em, Tiger."

But what about the writer who is able but unwilling? What about the difference between the cocky kid and the anxious old pro? The speeder and the bleeder? The highstrung and the low-key?

Flexible editors recognize, appreciate and take advantage of idiosyncrasy. Even when they share values and strategies, writers are diverse and quirky. To the extent that editors cultivate that diversity, they do their papers and their readers and themselves a favor.

But many editors are suspicious of quirkiness. They want good writing in their papers, but they can't stand their writers. Or understand them.

A reporter at a Texas newspaper circumnavigates the newsroom while he works on a story. When he's leaning on a file cabinet, he's working on a lead. If he's near the men's room, he's looking for a transition. And the desk gets ready when they see him near the water cooler, because he's heading for a kicker.

Donald Murray tells the story of a reporter at the Boston Globe who approached the desk near deadline.

> "How much time do I have?" the reporter asked his editor.
> "We want it in an hour."
> "Great," he said, looking at his watch. "I've got time for dinner."
> Murray followed him to the Globe cafeteria, watched him wolf down his supper and sit staring into space, his lips moving slowly for 10 minutes. Then the reporter returned to the newsroom and poured the story into the keys in nothing flat. Murray asked him later what he was doing while he sat staring in the cafeteria.
> "Rehearsing," he replied.

Even on deadline, it turned out, this veteran reporter needed the confidence that came from a little planning. The editor who watches reporters as they work learns that writing is filled with paradoxes. In this case, to write fast, you may have to write slow.

Most newswriters think they're weird and suffer guilt about their idiosyncrasies. To help them, editors must confront the problems of confidence that hamper the writer at each point in the writing process.

For example, most writers experience writer's block in some form, and many whip themselves because they procrastinate. Even veteran reporters believe that writing is magic and that only the gifted have the power.

When Roy Clark taught fifth-graders to write, he moved around the classroom to confer with the students. At times, an anxious child would throw her body across her paper to hide it from his view. "What immature behavior," he thought, until the day he approached a writer in a newsroom, and she turned down the gain control on her computer screen so he couldn't read her story.

Why do writers feel that way? Perhaps poet William Stafford expressed it best when he offered this advice for overcoming writer's block: lower your standards. Lower your standards? Is it possible that having high standards can hurt a writer?

When writers lower themselves into their chairs, they often project an idealized vision of how the story will come out: a dazzling lead, the dancing metaphors, flowing words, smiling prize juries. Then they lay their fingers on the keys, and the first words appear on the screen, words so far from their fantasy that the voice of the Internal Critic begins to whisper: "What an awful sentence, even worse than the one before it." "You'll never get this thing done." "You'll never be any good at this." Writers must learn, advised Dorothea Brande more than 50 years ago, to silence that voice during the early stages of writing while they build momentum, then to ungag that critical voice during revision, when its advice can do some good.

The editor must help during this complicated transaction. Short conferences between reporter and editor early in the process can help the writer build up steam. But neither writer nor editor should judge the first words on the screen too harshly. Later on, the editor can talk tougher. The editor's voice, blended with the voice of the writer's Internal Critic, should encourage the writer to apply the most exacting standards after the story is drafted.

Take the case of the writer who procrastinates. Such a writer causes a series of frustrating challenges for the editor, who waits and waits for something to happen, for some copy to flow. The writer may have all day or just an hour, but the drafting seems to take the same amount of time and always starts at the same time: late. "Why can't you draft early," snaps the impatient but still supportive editor, "so we have a chance to look at it and make it better?"

The editor may not see another of those writing paradoxes: inaction as a form of action. The writer who chain-smokes or paces or haunts the water fountain or arranges and rearranges the desk or stares into space may be preparing mentally for the act of writing, and may even be writing the story in his head.

Take the reporter who covers a fire at night and has a 15-minute ride back to the office, where she'll have to blast the story out on deadline. What happens in that reporter's head during the car ride back to the office? Since she can't write with her hands on the wheel, unless she's dictating into a tape recorder, she's probably drafting the story in her head, evaluating possible leads and getting herself pumped up for when she reaches her computer terminal.

Something writers and editors perceive as negative (procrastination) can be transformed into something positive (rehearsal). Good questions about form and content from the editor can get the writer's juices flowing and help the writer begin to make important decisions about the prospective story.

Sometimes, editors need to get reporters to change the way they work. But first, editors need to help reporters to understand how they do their best work, to get them to reflect on the methods they use and feel comfortable with those techniques. All writers have their tricks, and given the demands of daily journalism, they need them. But the combination of techniques and tricks must match the demands of the beat and the skills of the writer.

Acceptance of idiosyncrasy does not mean tolerance for sloppy work habits. The work of some writers would benefit from a reform of their

Coaching for Diversity

Most newsrooms in the United States are too white and too male, and that's too bad. A diverse newsroom would truly reflect the society it serves, enrich all journalists who work in it, serve readers of all kinds, expand our understanding of news, help us avoid dangerous stereotypes and clichés of vision, and give voice to the voiceless and power to the powerless.

Coaching helps editors create environments in which a diversity of journalists can do their best work. Whereas conventional editing treats everyone the same, usually badly, coaching recognizes the uniqueness of individuals and respects their differences. But coaching can also be abused as a weapon to support the biases of editors and to hammer flat the distinctive strengths and needs of individual reporters.

Mervin Aubespin, a veteran journalist at the Louisville Courier-Journal, spends considerable time coaching inexperienced reporters, especially minority journalists, and offers them career counseling. Aubespin takes this process seriously, remembering the day he, a black man, received a poor performance evaluation from his city editor because he was married to a white woman.

He also remembers the good work of his editor Bill Bridges, now a journalism educator, who helped Aubespin develop a distinctive voice in his writing. When they began working together, Bridges asked Aubespin to take him on a tour of a black neighborhood in Louisville and supported Aubespin's effort to write with passion about the history of Walnut Street, "the heart and soul of the black community."

"It's 5 p.m. on a brisk Friday in October," wrote Aubespin,

and the street is alive. Workers headed for home pause to chat outside the Mammoth Life Insurance building. Nat "King" Cole will be here in a few weeks, says the marquee of the Lyric Theater. Down the street, the voice of Jackie Wilson singing "Lonely Teardrops" drifts through the doorway of Davis's Record Shop. And still farther down, past Cricket the shoeshine man and the Kool Breeze Ice Cream Shop and the Liberty Cab Co., is Ralph's, where youngsters press their noses to greasy windows to see platters of "the best fried fish in town."

Aubespin remembers:

Bill was the only editor I knew who asked me to take him to an area of town to explain to him the dynamics of the neighborhood I lived in, which created a secret bond. While I had him in the car, I could expound on the things I'd like to do, the things I'd like to write about and do in my career. Following that, we became social friends. Most blacks find themselves out of the social circle at the places where they work. This opened up a situation for me. I could always discuss with him things I needed to know for my survival in the industry. As a result of that relationship, it put me in a position to know what was coming down the pike.

Aubespin recalls that Bridges developed a strong respect for Aubespin's approaches to stories:

Bill would tell me, "You know what is best, so you have to tell it in your own words." He recognized that storytelling has been a part of the black culture for years. I grew up in an environment where storytelling is a very natural thing with black people. He wouldn't let you go overboard, but he would pull it out of you.

During this process, Aubespin developed some ideas of how racism works in the newsroom and some survival skills on how to combat it. He passes these on to all reporters and editors:

Number one, when we come in, editors tend to assume that minority means inferior. Not only that, your colleagues assume it also, so you're working at a disadvantage from the start. So they approach us differently with that assumption. How quickly they take the story from you and rewrite it. They lose so much of the flavor and the rhythm.

The minority journalist has to make it clear not only that he accepts criticism but wants constructive criticism. On the other hand, the editor has got to make clear that there is no penalty for a writer who admits he has a problem and asks the editor to help him correct it.

I have seen cases where minority journalists have failed in this newsroom because they were afraid to admit they have a problem, and the editors were afraid to come to them to tell them that they had one. Sooner or later someone will get around to tell the person that things are just not working out, and we'll lose him. If a coaching relationship had been established at the very beginning, things could have been turned around.

methods, and the insightful editor finds ways to show different writers their weaknesses and strengths. A slow reviser may need to begin drafting early. A bland writer may have to learn to get better details into the notebook. A disorganized thinker may need to work from an outline. The good editor acts as if every writer, given supportive attention, can improve.

Vince Doria, former executive editor of The National, finds ways to talk to his "good soldiers." According to Doria,

> these reporters are doing a good job. They're working hard. I only have to keep in loose touch with them. What they're doing does not have to be my highest priority. But it's important to give them a little bit of time every week. Just enough to motivate them. Anything to let them know, "That was a real good story on such and such." It's important to be specific.

The opposite of good soldiers are "reluctant producers." Says Doria,

> They're very talented, but it's necessary to stay on them very close. If you give them an assignment on Monday that's due by Friday, you'd better be checking with them on Tuesday or Wednesday. Already, they'll be running into logistical problems. With them, you have to have a daily exchange. They are very valuable, but they can't always show up with the finished product.

The National had its share of "superstars," very talented reporters who, because of the quality of their work, have a high profile with readers. But, says Doria, you must not "take for granted what they do. You can't allow them to fall into a rut. Sometimes you have to send them to different kinds of events to write different kinds of stories."

Some writers aspire to be superstars but wind up as merely prima donnas. Doria finds them the toughest type to work with.

> They are talented, but they perceive their talent to be greater than it really is. It may take a serious closed-door-sit-down sort of thing to show them how they are being perceived by the rest of the staff. No one likes to be disliked or to appear selfish and self-centered. For whatever motivation, they'll clean up their act.

Lucille deView, an experienced editor and writing coach at the Orange County (Cal.) Register, preaches the value of working "not only with those writers having the most difficulty" but with all writers on the staff, beginning, intermediate and senior.

> Beginners often have unrealistic expectations and become easily discouraged. Offer constant reassurance that to become a polished, accom-

plished writer takes as much time and effort as it does to become a musician. Praise progress along the way. Do not overwhelm the beginner. Work on one flaw at a time.

The competent, intermediate, day-in-day-out writers may wish to be nudged into great things, to write Sunday features or be sent on major assignments. Show what improvements are needed to make this leap. Give practice assignments to do on their own time: a feature story, column or op-ed piece.

The senior writers are often the most humble, and the first to seek help. They may also be more insecure than beginners. Genuine approval and enthusiasm toward their work will give them the self-confidence they need to break fresh ground with their talents. If they have hit a plateau, they may want you to be tough, to fight with them, to give them blunt criticism some editors avoid out of awe or fear. They may be bored. Urge them to extend their reach. The feature writer might try an investigation; the sportswriter, an op-ed piece; the newswriter, a profile; the business writer, an essay.

The best editors, whether they know it or not, do informal writing research in their own newsrooms. They read the work of writers over time to identify patterns of strengths and weaknesses. One writer may clog the flow of stories with unnecessary attribution, a problem that a brief conference may solve. Another writer may overwrite, creating sentences overripe with competing images. This problem may take longer to solve, but the editor can persuade the writer that one interesting word or image in a sentence does more good work than several that compete for the reader's attention.

Foster Davis, as part of a writing improvement effort at the Charlotte Observer, collected the notebooks of his reporters and analyzed them. He was amazed and disturbed at what he discovered: first, that as much as 80 percent of the contents of the notebooks involved authorities speaking, that is, quotes from experts; second, that reporters wrote down very little from direct observation: few colors, images, sounds or concrete details. The limited content of the notebooks described by Davis almost insures conventional and superficial writing that lacks color, texture and context.

Editors should resist the urge to fix that which is not broken. An editor may not want to explore the working methods of a writer who is performing magnificently, except for the purpose of sharing them with other writers. On the other hand, a reporter with problems may benefit from a close analysis of his or her working methods by a curious and sympathetic editor.

Reading sentences aloud may help the unclear writer. The predictable writer may need inspiration from something new to read. Radically new assignments may benefit the burned-out writer. The inaccurate reporter may have to be called on the carpet. A refresher in libel law may reassure the columnist worried about hurting people.

Much of the editor's research into motivating writers results from rich conversations and careful listening. "Talking appears casual," says Lucille deView, "but is hard work and must be considered part of the editor's responsibilities. It is one way to pick up clues about what may be impeding a writer's progress."

But what about the things that impede an editor's progress? This chapter began with the notion that writers are idiosyncratic and that editors should adjust their coaching styles to meet diverse needs. Editors, of course, are just as diverse as writers. Few editors have been trained as coaches, few hired for their collaborative skills. They became editors, in many cases, because of their reporting expertise, which is admirable, unless that expertise can translate into narrow bossiness.

Editors who know how to coach and want to coach should be given the time and encouragement to do so. Editors who feel uncomfortable in a coaching role can delegate that responsibility to others, or they can rethink their attitudes and learn new skills to make their work easier and their newspapers better.

SUMMARY

- Respect the differences among writers.
- Adjust your coaching style to the needs of individual writers.
- Celebrate the offbeat and the quirky.
- Transform procrastination into rehearsal.
- Relax writers to overcome writer's block.
- Research the work habits of your own writers.
- Respect the differences among editors.

WORKSHOP

1. Write a narrative description of your own writing and/or editing behavior. Be sure to include any traits you think are distinctive. Don't be afraid to reveal your idiosyncrasies.
2. Many journalists are anxious about their writing and/or editing. Describe your own anxieties, and be as specific as possible. Do you fear failure, criticism, deadline pressure? Have a conversation with a friend, and share these fears. Try to find a way to relieve your friend's anxieties.

3. Working with a small group of writers or editors, select a topic to write on. Give yourself only 10 minutes to write. Each person then reads aloud his or her writing to the group. Try not to worry about your feeling that the piece is rough or imperfect. After the reading, each person in the group mentions one specific thing, even if it's only a word, that works in the piece.

4. Some writers say that they have to think about what they are going to say and then find the words to say it. Others say that they discover what they want to say by writing it. Which category do you fall into? Interview others on the same topic.

5. If there is one thing you could change about your writing or editing, what would it be? Now think carefully about this trait. Is it clearly a vice, or could it be a virtue in disguise? Discuss this idea with others.

6. Try to identify the fastest writers you know, the people who seem unaffected by procrastination and writer's block. Interview them about how they work quickly, and try to observe them in action.

7. Just for fun, write a short story on a blanked-out computer screen; most terminals let you darken the screen. You won't be able to evaluate or revise the words because you won't be able to see them. When you're through, write a brief description of this experiment; yes, you may brighten your screen.

8. Analyze the critical voice in your head as you read over one of your own stories. Is the voice mostly positive ("That's a dandy ending on that story") or negative ("That's the worst lead you've ever written"). Can you imagine controlling this voice, or does it control you?

PART THREE

Coaching the Writing Process

CHAPTER 7

Discovering the Writing Process

Editors learn writing processes by studying their own writing and by asking their writers questions about how they work. From such conversations, editors learn not just the splendid uniqueness of each writer, but also what writers have in common.

A 15-minute interview with each writer will help editors to understand much about how each writer works. These questions, among others, will help editors get to know their writers' writing processes:

- Are you a confident or an anxious writer?
- Are you fast or slow?
- Do you work from any kind of plan or outline?
- Do you take lots of notes?
- What percentage of your notes winds up in the story in some form?
- Do you spend lots of time on your lead?
- Do you have to perfect your lead before writing any other part of the story?
- Do you revise much?
- Do you get edited much?

Such an interview, buttressed by direct observation of a writer's work, reveals some paths along which writer and editor can travel together. Editors need to know enough about a writer's process to support what the writer does best and also to watch for trouble.

The editor learns that one writer is a good interviewer but never writes down what a person or place looks like. Another writer drafts slowly and fails to leave herself time to revise. Still another writes flabby sentences that need pruning and clarification. The editor who can see strengths and weaknesses in the process can coach the writer more effectively.

The new emphasis on the writing process in the newsroom may discomfort the editor who learned how to respond to a piece of writing with a red pencil. This negative tradition goes back a long way. Teachers still use writing as a form of punishment in many schools, and angry red marks on an essay can become a form of abuse.

Why do those red markings have so little impact on our writing, except to teach us to loathe it? We learn very little from the traditional bloodletting because many teachers and editors react only to the end product and not to the process that produced it. From their point of view, the whole writing process might look like this:

TURN IN DEFECTIVE COPY LATE

But most problems in a story can be traced to the steps in the process that produced them. And to improve our writing and the writing of others, we must look at the sequence of events and habits that make up the process for each individual.

Battered writers could draw up their own process diagrams, perhaps something like this:

- Avoid eye contact with editor.
- Find an idea.
- Have it rejected. Get assignment instead.
- Complain to another reporter.
- Begin to collect information.
- Panic when phone calls aren't returned.
- Type out notes for story.
- Call computer technician when system crashes.
- Take a slug from Maalox bottle.
- Listen to editor.
- Return to desk grumbling.
- Sit down and write lead.
- Give up. Get junk food from vending machine.
- Go to toilet. Smoke cigarette. Read graffiti and morning paper.
- Think of lead.
- Type lead.

- Type rest of story in 27 minutes.
- End story by stopping typing.
- Hand in story.
- Return to desk, make believe you're reading, but constantly look up to see expression on editor's face.
- Answer sarcastic questions from editor.
- Drive home.
- Worry.
- Fall asleep.
- Get phone call from copy editor.
- Argue to save ending. Lose argument.
- Go back to sleep.
- Get soggy paper off front lawn in morning.
- Open to story.
- Read a lead you didn't write.
- Decide not to read the rest.

A less comedic, and more naturalistic, description of the process may go something like this:

REPORT • TYPE • STALL • GRIT IT OUT

After talking with hundreds of writers and studying several models, Don Fry developed a diagram of the writing process that works for him, both as a template for his own writing and for explaining writing processes to others:

IDEA → REPORT → ORGANIZE → DRAFT → REVISE

The diagram proceeds through time from left to right, from selection of the story idea, to gathering information by reporting, through organizing this material, to preliminary drafting and final self-editing. After the *revise* step, he submits the final copy.

Actually, real writing does not involve this kind of linear progression through carefully demarcated steps. The selected topic changes as the writer reports it. The writer moves back and forth, turning from the keyboard to make just one more phone call. And the steps overlap; some reporters organize material while writing it down in a notebook. The diagram above captures only the essential sequence of steps, so keep the overlapping and circularity in mind. Later, we'll see some useful techniques that grow out of a tendency to backtrack.

Fry demonstrates the usefulness of this process model by showing how it helped him write a routine speech story quickly. As he describes his procedures, he draws analogies with the daily activities of beat reporters and mixes in some alternative techniques gathered from other writers. Fry's methods will seem cumbersome to some, but they work for him.

Fry begins with the *idea* stage, selecting the topic or having it assigned by an editor. As reporters, most of us write our best stories from our own story ideas, rather than from orders given by an assigning editor. We invest our own stories with our egos, as well as with our interest and energy. The best writing grows out of egotism, and we need to cultivate writing habits that draw on that self-centered interest without conflicting with the journalist's quest for objectivity or service to the reader.

When the desk gives us an assignment, we need to turn it into our own story idea, either by chatting with the editor or by brainstorming with ourselves. Sometimes, we discover the idea in the process of reporting it.

Some journalists believe that a reporter should form no preconceptions before arriving at the scene of a story, on the theory that preconceptions lead people to see only what they expect to see. But psychological research suggests the opposite. If people rehearse what they might encounter, they handle the eventual situation better. We talk better in a job interview if we practice answers ahead of time, even though we may not be asked any of the questions we rehearsed. The best reporters start thinking about leads, organization and endings on their way to the scene.

Fry covered a speech by Howard Troxler, then political columnist for the Tampa Tribune, at a local political club called Tiger Bay. Fry first read Troxler's columns from the previous week and that morning and then brainstormed with himself while driving to the speech. He expected Troxler to mock state politicians or Tampa problems, and he knew the audience would ask nasty questions about newspapers, a tradition whenever a journalist speaks in St. Petersburg. Fry hoped Troxler would say enough funny things to focus the story on one subject, rather than just delivering quips all over the place.

The *report* step follows *idea*. This story involved relatively simple reporting, just listening to the speech and getting a few reactions. Fry took five pages of notes and marked them up immediately afterwards. Selections from the notes appear below. Fry has cleaned the notes up just a little to make them more understandable.

Tiger Bay 7-10-90
Intro BY Herb Polson
Howard Troxler
drak blue suit, blac wing tips, "trademark" bowtie, round glasses, brown hair, blue shirt
NC, UNC, Tribune '82, Pasco Bureau,
    TallahaseE Bureau chIef

M-F column daily
"gossip, observation, . . .tidbits and humor"
state wide politiecs
'89 FPA 1st for cols,
finalist Green Eyeshade Award
favorite subjects: Helen Chavez, Jim Selby,
    Selvy PSC
same speech Tampa Tiger Bay several weeks ago
maybe ed board next
Troxler speaking
22KTT Pinls, 25K sndy
M-F Metro "Palm Tree Politics", Nov 1949
    title, started by Hampton Dunn 1958. . . .
DF (Send Stewart copies of Breeze.)
Hillsborough CC thanked Dunn for leaving
began col 1985, July 4
public regards him as wise because his
    picTURE appears in paper
will be reelected unless Dems get act
    together
polls increase as he backs away from taxes
Chiles - popular because of clean record
not convinced Chiles will get nomination
Nelson-"like guy HS always running for
    things". . . .
"Martinez will run negative campaign"
Nelson moving to left of Chiles, Martinez
    will kill him
If Chiles nominated, Martinez will run
    dirtiest campaign
40% Fla recognizes Chiles, BUT 900k new
    Republicans since he last ran.
Problems of Chiles:Depression, quit Senate,
    high-pay job, marijuana. . . .

Q3-Gary Slovick: does public care about
    issues? is Martinez dead?
"public forms visceral image of candidate"
"faith in electorate, elect who succeeds in getting message across". . . .
Q10-Zack Bowen: "Are you a communist?"
"Brand X newspaper is communist, we're simply liberal."
Q10-Don McBride: abortion?

Issue neutralized. Pro-Choice to responds immediate threat, Anti-
    Abortion ongoing.

Q11-Susanne Laurien: Martinez's staff,
    because of or in spite of Mac Stipanovich?
    CHECK SPELLING
Mac S = "something incarnate." "He is not
    evil, but simply amoral."
"He never feels bad for anything he does."
DF REVIEW AS THEATRE series of quips, not
    very funny
MS's goal is get Martinez elected
    president!!!!!!!
"The man is the gov, isn't he?". . . .
DIRTY CAMPAIGNING
"If I was manager of TT, I'm not
    sure I would have me writing a column."
Media sins: "not writing in English, not telling people what's going on"
<END NOTES>

Fry coded his notes by underlining and adding comments in the left margin:

	Tiger Bay 7-10-90
	Intro BY Herb Polson
	<u>Howard Troxler</u>
DESCRIPTION	drak blue suit, blac wing tips,
	"trademark" bowtie
OWL	round glasses, brown hair, blue shirt
DATE	NC, UNC, <u>Tribune '82</u>, Pasco Bureau,
	TallahaseE Bureau chIef
	<u>M-F column daily</u>
QY	"gossip, observation,. . .tidbits and
	humor"
	state wide politiecs
	'89 FPA [FLORIDA PRESS ASSOCIATION] 1st
	for cols, finalist Green Eyeshade Award
SPELLING?	favorite subjects: Helen Chavez, Jim
	Selby, Selvy PSC [PUBLIC SERVICE
	COMMISSION],
	same speech Tampa Tiger Bay several
	weeks ago
	maybe ed board next [EDITORIAL]
	Troxler speaking
?	22KTT Pinls, 25K sndy
TITLE OF COLUMN	M-F Metro "Palm Tree Politics",
	Nov 1949 title, started by Hampton
	Dunn 1958. . . .

	DF (Send Stewart copies of Breeze.)
	Hillsborough CC thanked Dunn for leaving
DATE	<u>began col 1985, July 4</u>
	public regards him as wise because his
	picTURE appears in paper

SUBJECT IS MARTINEZ

C BOTTOM	will be reelected unless Dems get act
LINE	together
	polls increase as he backs away from
	taxes
	<u>Chiles - popular because of clean record</u>
	not convinced Chiles will get nomination
QY	Nelson-"like guy HS always running for
	things". . . .
QC	<u>"Martinez will run negative campaign"</u>
	Nelson moving to left of Chiles,
	Martinez will kill him [= NELSON]
C KEY	If Chiles nominated, <u>Martinez will run dirtiest campaign</u>
	40% Fla recognizes Chiles, BUT 900k new
	Republicans since he last ran.
KEY	Problems of Chiles: <u>Depression, quit</u>
	<u>Senate, high-pay job, marijuana</u>. . . .
	Q3-Gary Slovick: does public care about
	issues? is Martinez dead?
C Q	"public forms visceral image of
	candidate"
C QY PK	"faith in electorate, elect who succeeds
	in getting message across". . . .
QY! PK	Q10-Zack Bowen: "Are you a communist?"
Q	"Brand X newspaper [ST. PETE TIMES] is
	communist, we're simply liberal."
	Q10-Don McBride: abortion?
	Issue neutralized. Pro-Choice to
	responds immediate threat, Anti-
	Abortion ongoing.
	Q11-Susanne Laurien: Martinez's staff,
	because of or in spite of Mac
	Stipanovich? CHECK SPELLING
Q KILL BABY	Mac S = "something incarnate." "He is
	not evil, but simply amoral."
Q	"He never feels bad for anything
	he does."

	DF REVIEW AS THEATRE series of quips, not very funny.
KEY QYY	MS's goal is get Martinez elected president!!!!!!
QYY KICKER!!!	"The man is the gov, isn't he?". . . .
THEME KEY	DIRTY CAMPAIGNING
Q KILL BABY	"If I was manager of TT [TAMPA TRIBUNE], I'm not sure I would have me writing a column."
Q	Media sins: "not writing in English, not telling peple what's going on"

Fry moves from the *report* stage to the *organize* stage when he feels he has "enough" to write the story. Experienced coaches find that most writing problems occur in the organizing stage. Many writers with problems simply skip any form of organization at all. Their training may teach them to do so, with its emphasis on lead writing. They move directly from reporting to grappling for a lead, and *then* decide what they want to say. Fry regards that sequence as backwards; he writes with assurance because he knows what he wants to say.

In the organizing phase, writers decide what they want to say. Fry performs this phase into four steps: marking up notes, spotting the high points, writing a point statement and sketching a plan. He spends less than 10 minutes on the entire organizational phase to allow time for drafting and editing, but that 10 minutes saves him hours and agony later.

First, Fry marks the notes to review their main points, to cement the important things in memory, and to mark things he may want to find later, such as numbers, names and the exact wording of quotations. Ideally, once he begins to type, he will not have to return to the notebook. Nothing distracts writers more than flipping through those blurry pages.

Don eliminates things in the notebook that he does not expect to use in the story. In talking to the best reporters, we find that only about 5 percent of their notes eventually appear in the story in some form. Marking the notes allows reporters to discard around 75 percent of the material; whatever gets no mark simply vanishes.

Reporters mark their notes in ways that suit their personalities. Some slow writers don't mark the notebook at all. Some just put a check in the margin beside good stuff. At the other extreme, some reporters categorize their notes, index them and sort them by computer.

As you can see from his notes, Fry uses a moderately complicated coding system, underlining important things and scribbling comments in the left margin. Because he tends to write from the quotations, he puts a *Q* for

Quotation, in the margin beside every one and adds a *Y,* for *Yes,* beside important quotations. So, *QY* means "a good quote" likely to make it into the story. The most important ideas get *KEY* in the margin.

Fry distinguishes his own ideas from the source's by putting his initials (*DF*) in the margin. He once wrote a great piece that turned on one key quotation, so he called up the source just to check the exact wording of this important quotation. The source verified the wording, but added, "By the way, *you* said that, not me." After that near-disaster, Fry carefully distinguished his own ideas. That marking also helps prevent accidental plagiarism caused by mistaking other people's ideas for his own.

Further down, we see this note: "C QY PK 'faith in electorate, elect who succeeds in getting message across'"—*QY* marks a good quotation, and *PK* indicates a potential kicker, or ending. Fry decides to center his story on the gubernatorial campaign, so he puts a *C* in the margin beside anything that concerns that campaign.

Finally, Fry writes this note: "Q KILL BABY 'If I was manager of TT [TAMPA TRIBUNE], I'm not sure I would have me writing a column.'" The *Q* indicates a quotation. But this quotation has nothing to do with the story, so Fry marks it *KILL BABY* so that he won't get carried away and warp the story to get the precious quotation in.

Fry continues organizing by seeking his main ideas. He sets the notes aside and spots the big ideas by talking aloud to himself and scribbling down whatever strikes him, like this:

SCRIBBLE SHEET
DIRTY CAMPAIGNING ESP TV
WHAT TIGER BAY IS
DEMS CRUMMY
CHILES VS NELSON
WHAT MARTINEZ WILL DO ← STIPANOVICH
LOCAL - STEWART - NO

These scribbles tell Fry what strikes him in the material, what sits at the top of his mind. Then he uses a technique of asking two focusing questions, taught to him by Christopher Scanlan of Knight-Ridder: "What's this about?" and "What's my point?" For hard news stories, we could modify the first question to "What's the news here?" Fry answered the two questions like this:

What's this about? Troxler predicted the dirtiest gov. campaign in Florida history.
What's my point? Press and polling have created a monster.

These statements differ in intent. "What's this about?" describes the content, while "What's my point?" tells the theme of the piece. Fry answers the questions in writing as precisely as possible, to show him what he wants to say and what he wants his reader to remember.

The second question, "What's my point for my reader?," produces a theme or thesis statement, a ruling idea that will give Fry's ideas shape and force. Notice the egotistical pronouns: "What's *my* point for *my* reader?" As we shall see later, the point statement Fry wrote for this story proved not pointed enough, and he could have written faster if he had been more precise at this stage. But it got him started.

The point statement tells Fry what he thinks and also gives him a test for including or excluding materials. *Anything that does not help make the point does not go in the story.* And here we reach the heart of news reporting and writing. Reporters tend to think of their craft in terms of cramming stuff into limited space, but as Donald Murray says, "The secret of brevity is selection, not compression." Reporters invest the material they collect with their egos, and they don't want to throw any of it out. They want to get it all into the story.

The following scenario has happened to everybody at least once: You've brought back the best quote of your career, perhaps the best quote in the history of journalism. It's short, punchy, has a great pun in the middle, and was spoken by an important source. There's only one thing wrong with it: it has nothing to do with the story! So what do you do? Naturally you warp the story to get it in, and your story turns into a shapeless mess.

The point statement becomes a sword for killing the great but irrelevant fact, quote or anecdote. Because writers have an almost maternal attachment to such material, Fry calls this procedure "killing the babies."

Drawing the organizing phase to a close, Fry now knows what he wants to say. So, he writes a plan, a roadmap for the parts of the story. Plans involve a label, just a code word or two for each section, fewer than 10 words in all, no more. The plan simply lists the parts and their order. Fry wrote this plan:

LEAD: STRAIGHT

1. WHY DIRTIEST

2. MARTINEZ NOW

3. CAMPAIGN

4. LOCAL

KICKER: PRESIDENCY!

This plan lists four parts framed by a lead and a kicker. Fry designed it by asking what the reader needs to know and in what order. He writes the plan down so he won't forget it or get drawn off by attractive materials into writing something quite different. The total time expended in organizing all these materials came to about five minutes. That five minutes later saved Fry an hour, because he knew what he wanted to say.

With this plan in hand, Fry moves from *organize* to *draft*. He drafts very quickly, paying little attention to the finish of the piece or even to spelling and grammar. He tries not to revise as he goes along because he wants to produce a whole draft as quickly as possible. Most newswriting sags in the middle because writers get tired or rushed or lost. They spend 20 minutes crafting a lead, then an hour getting the first half just right, and then blast through the rest in 10 minutes to make the deadline. Hence the sagging middle. By writing a first draft as quickly as possible from a plan, Fry spends the same amount of time on the second half as on the first, and he doesn't get tired.

Fry wrote the following draft, coached two reporters, attended a short meeting and took two phone calls, all in 75 minutes:

Troxler Predicts Dirtiest Governor Campaign*

Howard Troxler, the Tampa Tribune's sharptongued political columnist, predicted the dirtiest campaign for govrnor in Florida's history.

Troxler spoke before a crowd of about 150 people at the July 10th meeting of the Pinellas County TIger Bay CLub in St. Petersburg. Tiger Bay sponsors speakers on political subjects, and the audience delights in asking barbed questions.

Disorganized Dems

Troxler sketched a scenario that assumes the Dem Party's inability to mount successful campaigns. "Demcorats are such horrible campaigners," he said. He pictured Democratic politicians saying, "Let's find the most inofensive candidate we can, and demand that people vote for him."

He expects a lively Democratic primary, with Bill Nelson attacking Lawton Chiles vigorously. Troxer sees Nelson as "like the guy you knew in High School who was always running for everything." So far, Chiles has maintained such a low profile that Nelson has not damaged him. Troxler sees no clear winner in the Democratic primaries.

Media Martinez

Troxler, sporting his trademark bow tie and owlish glasses over a hopeful blue shirt and fundamental blue suit, says that "Martinex has spent his entire

*Mistakes preserved in draft.

administration constructing good 30-second issues." The governor, according to Troxler, dishes up 1 mini-issue at a time and then asks, "Do you like me now"

The audience, mostly conservatively dressed local business men, reacted to the columnist's quips with mild titters. (One later asked him if he was a Communist).

Troxler says that the Martinez administration "runs the government by polls," and they respond to criticism by citing surveys.

Troxler thought that Nelson will portray himself as left of the mildly Centrist Chiles; if Nelson's tactics prevail, Martinez will then atack him as a far-out Liberal. If Nelson's strategy fails, Troxler expects the Martinez forces to mount the nastiest media campaign in history, with Ted Bundy domnating the screen.

Dirt on the Tube

Troxler sees Chiles as popular because of his long, clean record as u.s. Senator. He expects Martinez commercials to focus on Chiles's treatment for depression, quitting the Senate, accepting a high-paying job immediately afterwards, and his admission of having smoked marijuana. "Chiles's halo," said TRoxler, "will fade as he campaigns.

He expects Martinez to continue the type of commercials his staff aired in MAy. The audience laughed as he reminded them of a 30-sec spot showing the governor strolling on a beach while a dolphin jumped in the background. "Did you notice that Martinez was wearing shoes?" he quipped.

Locals Nicer

After the meeting St. Petersburg Vice Mayor Robert Stewart said he did not expect such dirty television campaigning ever to infect local politics. He characterized city elections as "neighbors running against neighbors."

Stewart thinks that local politicians cannot use such tactics "because we're so close to the people, because we live in those neighborhoods." He said, with a grin, that his opposition satisfies itself with tearing up his campaign signs.

Tomorrow the World

Troxler sees goals for the Martinez staff beyond just a second term. He believes that Max Stipanovich, the governor's campaign manager, intends to win the U.S. presidency for Bob Martinez.

The audience sucked in its breath. The U.S. presidency for Bob Martinez! Troxler then added, "The man is the governor, isn't he?"

Fry does the final step, *revise*, in two passes. First, he reads the piece aloud, taking no notes and making no corrections, touching the keys only to scroll the pages. He gets a sense of the piece as a whole, experiences how long the passages might seem to the reader, and hears where the rhythms clash. Many writers say they read their pieces over in revision, but they're too self-conscious to read them aloud. Fry reads aloud so he can hear every word, can discover where the little words bump into each other and destroy the rhythm. When we read silently, we jump across the phrases and don't sound out those little words.

Then Fry crawled through the text on the screen and made all the little changes for sense, grace, rhythm and finish. This draft turned out pretty clean, and Fry mostly mopped up the typos.

Fry had plenty of time until deadline, but he felt that somehow the piece lacked "shape." The sentences flowed, but the ideas didn't so he asked Roy Clark to read the piece and coach him.

Clark: All right, I've read it. How can I help you?

Fry: Well, Troxler didn't give a very good speech, so I decided to write about his serious message, that the campaign is going to be dirty. I think my story's pretty clear, but it doesn't capture the way that it sounded.

Clark: I read some of that tension in the story. You've got in the lead, I think, a really good hook. I assume he was sort of all over the map.

Fry: Oh yeah. I'm only reporting about 10 percent of what he said. He was just slinging quips all over the place, trying to be funny and not landing. Typically for me, the lead is very straight, but that lead doesn't hint at any of the fun.

Clark: Okay, but I'm less concerned with that. It's a strong lead: He "predicted the dirtiest campaign for governor in Florida's history." I'm ready to read more, and you support the lead later. But next I've got a paragraph on Tiger Bay, which is just background.

Fry: Do you think that graph is too high?

Clark: Well, possibly. Maybe the part about how "the audience delights in asking barbed questions" could go down here where you're talking about the audience response.

Look what you've got. You've got a lead about the dirtiest campaign ever, then you've got two subsections on "Disorganized Democrats" and "Media Martinez," then we get "Dirt on the Tube." I don't think you've shown me enough information about how this is going to be the dirtiest campaign. You've surfaced that as an interesting and dominant element. Would it be possible to just make that the top third of the story, and then take a step back and background it with the "Disorganized Democrats" and "Media Martinez?"

Fry: Sure, I *can* do that, but I don't like to write a boring inverted pyramid. I thought of the lead as a mystery hook to hold the reader for a while. Now, I want to make sure that the two sections ahead of "Dirt on the Tube" are interesting enough to pull the readers all the way down.

Clark: I don't think so. For me, backgrounding material usually takes a subordinate role, because by definition, it's a little bit less interesting.

Fry: That's inverted-pyramid thinking. I tend to lead *up to* things, rather than *down from* them.

Clark: Yeah, okay, but this story, it seems to me, might lend itself a little bit more to pyramid style. Remember that you've got a couple of nice nuggets toward the end, and you've got a real strong kicker, which will give the piece a sense of closure that you don't get in a typical pyramid.

I think maybe, if you're worried about structure, you need more . . . more . . .

Fry: More dirt on top?

Clark: More dirt up high. A couple of other questions. Do you have anything, anybody commenting on the speech? This thing about the local election, though I'm interested in it, seems slightly out of focus.

Fry: Yeah, I thought so too.

Clark: I'm interested in it, but it's not what Troxler was talking about. I'm interested in somebody talking about either Troxler or the Martinez campaign. Do you have anybody in your notes at all?

Fry: No, I was just trying to localize a state story.

Clark: I think the way you do that is not by taking this dirty campaign thing and moving it to the local level, but by getting some local person to comment on the state issue.

Fry: I think so too, but I don't have that, and I can't get it this late.

Clark: Well, in that case, I'd take it out and make the piece shorter, which would probably be a more appropriate length for a fairly mediocre speech.

Fry: Then I have a speech story with no reaction. Oh well. Do you think I ought to punch it up and try to make it a little funnier, a little brighter?

Clark: Well, I think you've got something strong at the end, and I also like the way you described Troxler. I've never seen Howard Troxler, but you take me into the room and show me what he looks like.

Fry: Would you like to see him some more?

Clark: Well, what did he do that was interesting?

Fry: Nothing.

Clark: Well, then, no.

Fry: Okay. I like your structural suggestions. I was having trouble with that. Thanks.

Clark: Well, let's see what the next draft looks like.

Fry didn't write another draft; he quickly revised the previous one into final copy by rearranging the parts and punching up the sentences, as follows:

Finally Final
Columnist Predicts Dirty Governor Campaign

By Don Fry

Howard Troxler, the Tampa Tribune's razor-tongued political columnist, predicted the dirtiest campaign for governor in Florida's history.

Speaking before the Tiger Bay Club Thursday, Troxler announced his subject as "Why Governor Martinez Can't Win the Election, and Why He Probably Will."

Dirt on the Tube

Troxler expects a lively Democratic primary, with Bill Nelson vigorously attacking Lawton Chiles. He predicts that Nelson will portray himself somewhat to the left of the mildly centrist Chiles. If Nelson wins the primary, Martinez will picture him in television spots as a far-out liberal.

If Nelson loses, Troxler expects the Martinez forces to mount the nastiest media campaign in history, trying to blacken Chiles' long, clean record in the U.S. Senate. Troxler thinks Martinez will focus on Chiles' treatment for depression, resignation from the Senate, acceptance of a high-paying job immediately afterwards, and admission of having smoked marijuana. "Chiles' halo," said Troxler, "will fade as he campaigns."

Bundy and Horton

Regardless of who wins, images of serial killer Ted Bundy will dominate the screen, Troxler thinks, reminiscent of President George Bush's Willie Horton spots.

Troxler also expects Martinez to continue the fuzzy commercials his staff dreamed up in May. The audience giggled as he reminded them of a 30-second spot showing the governor strolling on a beach while a dolphin jumped merrily in the background. He quipped: "Did you notice that Martinez was wearing shoes?"

Troxler spoke before about 150 of the 800 members of the Suncoast Tiger Bay Club at their July 10 meeting in St. Petersburg. The non-partisan club sponsors speakers on political subjects, and the audience competes to ask the meanest question.

Disorganized Democrats

Troxler assumed the Democratic Party's inability to mount successful campaigns. Democrats," he said, "are such horrible campaigners." He imagined Democratic politicians thinking, "Let's find the most inoffensive candidate we can, and demand that people vote for him."

Troxler pictures the photogenic Nelson as "like the guy you knew in high school who was always running for everything." So far, Chiles has maintained such a low profile that Nelson has not damaged him. No one, Troxler thinks, can predict a clear winner.

Media Martinez

Troxler, sporting his trademark bow tie and owlish glasses over a hopeful blue shirt and fundamental blue suit, says that the Martinez administration "runs the government by polls," responding to criticism by citing opinion surveys. They use television spots to affect those polls.

Troxler says that "Martinez has spent his entire administration constructing good 30-second issues." The governor, according to Troxler, dishes up one mini-issue at a time, and then asks, "Do you like me now?"

The audience, mostly conservatively dressed local businesspeople, reacted to the columnist's quips with mild titters, although one questioner asked Troxler if he was a Communist.

Tomorrow the World

Troxler thinks the Martinez staff has ambitions beyond just a second term. He believes that Mac Stipanovich, the governor's campaign manager, intends to make Martinez president of the United States. The stunned audience sucked in its breath. Troxler added, "The man *is* the governor, isn't he?"

Fry knew he had a problem with structure, but he couldn't figure it out. Notice that he even dodged the issue when Clark asked what he needed help on. Clark got Fry back on track by asking questions about organization when Fry couldn't revise successfully.

If Fry had found himself unable to write a suitable lead, Clark would have moved him from drafting back to organizing. If Fry had had difficulty in organizing, Clark might have asked if he had collected the right information in the reporting stage. If the reporting had gone poorly, Clark might have questioned the story idea. Note the general principle: solve the problem by moving one stage back in the writing process.

Editors can use a writing-process model to help their reporters. A reporter comes to the desk and complains of trouble in writing a lead. The old-style editor responds, "What's wrong with you? You write leads for a living." And the writer falls to the floor, gutted for that day. Consider this alternative: question the writer to find out exactly where in the process things have broken down. Take a step back to evaluate the material collected by the reporter, searching always for a good lead.

Finally, a reminder about idiosyncrasy. Fry's writing process fits his very organized personality: he thinks by planning and likes to know what he's doing before he does it. His colleague Clark prefers to discover his topic by writing about it. Some writers think about organization by writing leads, sometimes 30 or 40 of them. One writer scribbles all his quotations on cards and sorts them on his office floor.

All methods are legitimate, if they work for the writer. We offer Fry's writing process, not as a model, but as a framework for others to discover their own best methods.

SUMMARY

- Use the steps: *idea, report, organize, draft, revise.*
- If you get stuck, look for the problem one step earlier in the process.
- Help writers to develop strengths in each of the steps and to change habits that slow them down.
- Remember that the process differs according to the individual's personality, work habits and job.

WORKSHOP

1. Interview three writers, using the list of questions on p. 60. Based on these interviews, compose a "writer's profile" of each reporter. At the end of each profile, describe how an editor might support the work of that writer. Have someone interview you, using the same process.
2. Draw a writing-process diagram of how you work. Use a large sheet of paper and colored markers. Be creative and have fun. When you are finished, hang it on the wall and talk about it with others.
3. Professional journalists laugh with recognition when they see the parody of the writing process on p. 61–62. Discuss the truths behind the parody. What forces in the newsroom demoralize writers?
4. Study and analyze Don Fry's discussion of his own writing process. Fry thinks of himself as a highly organized writer. Do you agree? What surprises you about the way he works? If you were his editor, how would you work with him?
5. With a friend, play the roles of Don Fry and his editor talking about the Troxler story *before* he organizes it into a draft. Swap roles. Would these conversations have saved Fry from structural problems?
6. With a friend, play the roles of Don Fry and his editor. Conduct a five-minute writing conference, using his rough draft (p. 70–71) as your text. Switch roles.
7. Read at least a dozen stories in today's newspaper. Using a model of the writing process, analyze where you think each piece is strong or weak. For example: One story may be based on a strong *idea*, but is not supported by sufficient *reporting*. Another may have good *organization*, but need additional *revision*.
8. Using these same 12 stories, think of one question that you would ask each writer to help him or her improve the work.
9. Notebooks are private, like a dog's tail. But see if you can get some reporters to share with you their notebooks and their systems for mapping the notes. Which systems seem most efficient to you?
10. With a friend, read aloud Clark's conference with Fry to see how long it took. Does anything in this conversation surprise you? What would you have done differently?

CHAPTER 8

Coaching for Ideas

On June 13, 1948, Babe Ruth, dying of cancer, made his final appearance at Yankee Stadium. Nat Fein, a photographer for the New York Herald Tribune, shot this photo that won him a Pulitzer Prize and a place in baseball history.

What makes Fein's picture special? Its composition moves many people: the huge figure of Ruth in the foreground, leaning on his bat as if it were a cane, his hat off, head slightly bowed. His teammates stand to one side, hats over hearts as a band plays "Auld Lang Syne." In the background, out of focus, the unmistakable façade of the stadium itself, the house that Ruth built, frames the huge crowd. In front of all this stands the number 3, the symbol of the most famous baseball player of all time.

Why did the other 25 photographers at the stadium that day fail to take that memorable shot? Where did Fein's counterintuition and creative vision come from? What inspired him to step away from his fellow photographers and move behind Ruth to capture the emotion of the moment?

Answering those questions would unlock the secrets of true talent. We have Fein's testimony that the coaching he received from his picture editor, Richard Crandell,

enhanced his original vision. "Whenever you can," Crandell exhorted, "make your pictures without flashbulbs. Natural light catches the mood of the occasion."

The day was overcast, but Fein, his editor's words ringing in his ears, compensated for the dull light. He shot the great photo from behind Ruth without a flash. And there, captured forever in the lower-right corner of the photograph, like a fly in amber, as if in tribute to Fein's creativity, squats another photographer who won no prize that day. The poor stiff shoots from the front with a flashbulb.

Creative vision, the original story idea or fresh angle, happens when the supportive editor nurtures the talented journalist.

The great journalists, whether reporters or editors, see the world as a storehouse of story ideas. They have a form of X-ray vision that allows them to see human action behind the thick walls of faceless institutions. They are curious about everything, fascinated with how things work, and live to uncover secrets.

Unfortunately, not all editors foster an environment in which such journalism can take root. Some editors impose all story ideas on writers. They want to control the news, limit it to safe subjects and find comfort in the most conventional approaches to writing and reporting. Reporters who work for such editors suffer, as do their readers. Over time, these writers' reporting muscles atrophy. They forget how to see and hear; they just execute orders.

Another kind of editor turns the newsroom into an idea factory, where the act of searching for new definitions of news, and for new ways of telling stories, becomes the essential journalistic activity, a mode of conversation, a form of vision. These editors generate many good ideas themselves but also want lots of ideas percolating up from reporters. "Keep your eyes and ears open," they tell reporters. "Let me know what's happening. Help me to see what's going on out there."

Openness to ideas is an editor's great gift to a writer, but becoming a receptive editor is more complicated than it sounds. Writers often have many more ideas than they can execute. Some writers testify that they get 10 story ideas for every one that gets reported. So, helpful editors need to become sounding boards, matching their knowledge of their writers against the ideas. Responses like these to writers' ideas prove particularly helpful:

> Which of these ideas really turns you on?
> Which of these are you ready to do now?
> I'd really like to see us do this one. Let me know when you're ready.
> What kind of reporting will be necessary to do that right?
> How much time do you think you'll need?
> Can you think of a way to do that story that hasn't been tried before?
> I announced at the editors' meeting that you're working on that, but
>   if the story turns out differently, don't hesitate to let me know.
> How can I help you get this done?

Here are some less helpful, even deadly, responses:

> You're just full of ideas, aren't you?
> We don't have time to be thinking about those stories. You've got to
>   cover X.
> Don't come to me with an idea unless you're prepared to do it.

But I already announced at the editors' meeting that the story was
   going to be about X.

I'll tell you when I need help finding story ideas.

That's a good idea, but I'm going to give it to Sarah. She's good on
   those kinds of stories.

Where do good story ideas come from? From everywhere. They come
from reporters and assigning editors, of course, but also from publishers
and their friends, from copy editors, secretaries, security guards, printers,
readers and sources. Any idea can and should be considered. Real openness means that no idea is inherently bad. A story concept that seems to
lead through dense jungles and impenetrable thickets may become the
only path to lost cities and buried treasures.

Newspapers, your own and your competitor's, are the most important
source of story ideas. Newspapers brim over with underdeveloped stories,
announcements of meetings and events, tiny clues that could lead to
interesting narratives.

One day, Roy Clark read an announcement in the paper about a
young minister who planned to spend the weekend preaching from a little
house built atop a telephone pole. He called it his "pole-pit" and invited
everyone to hear him preach the Gospel from on high.

Clark rushed down to interview the minister. As soon as he arrived at
the church, Clark understood what this event was all about. The church
shared a street with about a dozen other churches. Clark had a story about
the town's competition for souls and could judge the preacher's publicity
stunt in that light. One little announcement in the paper sowed the seed
for a terrific story.

Time defeats many good ideas, but editors must encourage reporters
not to give up, in the shadow of deadline, the search for an interesting
angle. When adrenalin, the journalist's drug, kicks in, the reporter can
strive for something special in a story, even if only an image or an interesting word. The editor must create an environment in which even average
assignments can become surprisingly good stories.

Supportive editors should inspire reporters to take the most routine
assignments and turn them into interesting stories that become models
for the genre. Each year, a reporter at the St. Petersburg Times must cover
the annual spelling bee because the newspaper co-sponsors it. But few
embrace the story with the kind of energy that Bill Nottingham felt when
he wrote this lead: "Thirteen-year-old Lane Boy is to spelling what Billy the
Kid was to gunfighting: icy-nerved and unflinchingly accurate."

Secret stories lurk even in the press release describing the new telephone book. When Clark got that dreaded assignment, he challenged him-

self to turn the lemon into a triumph. First, he thought about a book review, imagining the phone book as having more characters than a Russian novel, but no plot. Someone suggested that he call the first name listed in the book, but it turned out to be "AAAA Roofing," followed by all the businesses with AAA initials. Perhaps there was a business story there somewhere.

But then he looked up the last name in the book: "Z. Zyzor." "What a strange name," he thought, and wondered about life at the bottom of every alphabetical listing.

Clark called the number and got the cafeteria of the local post office. He dialed again and got the same number. No one knew any Z. Zyzor. Using the city directory, he discovered that, indeed, the address next to the name was that of the post office. He called the personnel department, but got nowhere.

When he had almost given up hope, he got a call from the postmaster: "I hear you've been asking about Z. Zyzor."

Finally, he told Clark the story. Back in 1948, the letter carriers decided to pitch in money to get a telephone installed at the post office for their personal use. They invented the name Z. Zyzor and told their families: "If you need me in an emergency, just call the last number in the book."

That's how a story about the new phone book made the front page of the local section on a busy news day.

But what if your reporters are not so ingenious, what if they have learned, perhaps from bad editors, to see news and the world in the most conventional ways? What kind of coaching will help them open their eyes and ears? The following approaches have worked.

Find the person behind the story and the story behind the person. A follow-up to a story about a postal-rate increase became a tale about the unpopularity of postal clerks. The story began with this lead: "When Marion W. McDonald went to work for the postal service back in 1945, you could mail a letter for 3 cents and a postcard for a penny." This scene follows a description of the rate increases:

> "Shakespeare could explain why the post office gets such bad press," said McDonald to a reporter. "Do you remember Marc Antony's words over the body of Julius Caesar?"
>
> The reporter looked down at his notes like a nervous schoolboy.
>
> McDonald peered hard into the reporter's eyes. His forum was framed by scales, meters and postal charts. He spoke his lines accurately and with conviction: "The evil that men do lives after them; the good is oft interred with their bones."

Clark was fascinated and delighted by the postal worker who quoted Shakespeare, and wanted his readers to share that same experience.

Go one step beyond what is expected. Clark reviewed "Midnight Express," a powerful film about a young American trapped in a brutal Turkish prison. Some other reviewers wondered whether the film had been unfair to the Turkish people, depicting them as torturers and sadists.

Clark felt the need to go one step beyond the review, which led to a column idea. He telephoned the Turkish deputy ambassador to the United Nations. "For years we've been stereotyped as being brutal, terrible, the mustachioed, scimitar-bearing people," said Altemur Kilic. "Unfortunately, this film uses all the tricks in the book to come out against the Turkish people. As an American, when you come out of the movie house, you come out with hatred against the Turks, not with hatred against the Turkish prison system. If I were paranoiac, I would say there was Greek or Armenian money behind it."

The editor should always teach the new reporter, and remind the veteran, that he or she can reach anyone in the world on the telephone at almost any time, and that making just one more call may give you what you need for a great story.

Don't be afraid to use your life as a mirror of some larger reality. In the days before Madonna and MTV, Clark tried to protect his daughters from Barbie dolls. "I hate Barbie," he wrote. "I hate her grown-up polyethylene breasts, her glamorously expensive outfits, her superstar image, her camera, her microphone, her motor home, her sports car, her bedroom set and especially her blond boyfriend Ken with his rose-tinted sunglasses, his mink coat and his suede jumpsuit."

Clark checked the clips and found the name of another man who hated Barbie. He lived in Oakland, Oregon, and Clark found him through directory assistance. Bill Barton disapproved of the way Mattel was marketing Barbie. He worried that she was too sexy and flashy for little girls and that she was being advertised in a way that conditioned little kids to be aggressive consumers. What makes Barton's criticism of Barbie relevant? He invented her.

Editors should remind reporters that journalists live in the world too and that their experiences may lead to legitimate story ideas. Perhaps there are suddenly a number of houses on your block for sale. Or garbage trucks are tearing up your street. Or it seems that traffic problems make getting to work more difficult. Or you can't find places to park downtown. While reporters should avoid the conflict of interest in writing a story that offers them personal advantage, they could assume that their problems and concerns may be shared by many other citizens. They need to learn to see their community through the citizens' eyes.

To the tuned-up journalist, even nothing can become something. Clark noticed that the local bluenoses failed to raise a protest about the arrival of the musical "Oh! Calcutta!":

> Like the floozy she is, "Oh! Calcutta!" will strut her stuff into town this week, spend the night and move on.
>
> The controversial nudie musical makes its first St. Petersburg appearance in a one-night stand at 8 p.m. Wednesday at the Bayfront Center.
>
> Although the play faces protest from some church and community leaders in other Florida cities, such as Melbourne and Lakeland, "Oh! Calcutta!" comes to St. Petersburg without a whimper of opposition.

When Clark learned that protest groups had attacked the play in other Florida communities, he assumed that they would turn out in full force in St. Petersburg. He prepared to write a story about it. At first he was disappointed when there was no outcry, but then he realized that the lack of protest broke the trend, providing him with an even better story. Nothing became something.

Great features writers and their editors cultivate an eye for the offbeat. John McPhee of the New Yorker wrote a piece on Atlantic City by visiting the locations mentioned on the Monopoly board, including Jail. He also once went foraging through the woods looking for things to eat with Ewell Gibbon, the late naturalist.

Jeff Klinkenberg learned the value of an offbeat perspective at the Miami News, a spunky afternoon paper always looking for a fresh angle on a story. Klinkenberg watched sportswriter Al Levine find Dolphin quarterback Earl Morrall's barber, the only guy in town who, in an era of long hair, knew how to give a genuine flattop. Klinkenberg later became an outdoors writer for the St. Petersburg Times, doing profiles of every one-legged fisherman on Tampa Bay. He once found a young man who set up a Nerfball fantasy basketball league in his own garage:

> By day he is the mild-mannered vice president of a small family business which stuffs plastic bags with nuts and bolts. At night, on the basketball court, things are different. Terry Lewis, 20, is a superstar. . . . It's only a one-man basketball league. The applause rings only in his imagination. But Terry Lewis has scored 25,000 points in 780 games in his garage-turned-gym. He's a holy terror.

Concrete objects can inspire story ideas. An old army medal in a drawer inspires a reminiscence. A piece of sheet music becomes a story on its composer. A high school yearbook becomes a window onto 20 years of educational change.

Some of the most thoughtful journalists can predict trends just as they gain momentum. A waitress takes an order not on a pad but on a handheld computer. A small public school is established at a large GE plant. Little kids collect baseball cards not for fun but for investment. Suddenly a spark of narrative appears before the writer's eyes.

But good writers also go against the grain, avoiding what Donald Murray calls "clichés of vision." People with disabilities are not always heroic. Women and old people are not always victims. Capitalists can be altruistic. Some writers even develop strong counterintuitive sensibilities about the news in their own paper. They wait and watch, weigh the evidence, and find another way.

Mary Jo Melone, a columnist in the Tampa bureau of the St. Petersburg Times, saw the business community falling all over itself at the prospect of New York developer Donald Trump taking an interest in Tampa construction. Her coach had taught her about "contrarian thinking," looking the opposite way from the pack. Driving through downtown Tampa one day, she watched a homeless man cross the street. Suddenly, she asked herself, "What do the homeless think of Donald Trump?" Bingo!

Many of these attitudes come from a rich life of reading. Sadly, too many journalists fail to read their own papers, but the smart ones scour their papers for new ideas and angles. They might spend an afternoon poring through magazines in the library. They wisely read books that carry them beyond the boundaries of their special interests. Their reading helps them see the world through many lenses.

In many ways, the search for the great story idea is a little like prayer. Before you get an answer, you have to ask a question. You may look deep within yourself. Or make appeals to the Muses. Or, better yet, seek the help and advice of a supportive editor.

SUMMARY

- Find the person behind the story and the story behind the person.
- Go one step beyond what is expected.
- Don't be afraid to use your life as a mirror of some larger reality.
- To the tuned-up journalist, even nothing can be something.
- Great feature writers and their editors cultivate an eye for the offbeat.
- Concrete objects can inspire story ideas.
- Some journalists can predict trends just as they gain momentum.
- Go against the grain.

WORKSHOP

1. Walk around with a photographer or artist. Have him or her talk about what he or she "sees," those details or scenes that he or she finds visually

interesting. Walk around again by yourself, this time carrying a camera. Look for unusual sights or perspectives and snap pictures of them. Don't worry about the quality of the photos you produce (film is optional). Let the viewfinder open your eyes.

2. Make another walking tour, this time with a reporter. Ask him or her if he or she "sees" any interesting story ideas or anything that piques his or her curiosity. Take another walk on your own, this time with your notebook instead of a camera. Write down anything that interests you.

3. Read today's newspaper, and watch the evening news show. Make a list of stories that are insufficiently covered or announcements that might be developed into full stories.

4. Spend some time in the library reading through current periodicals. Make a list of the story ideas that you could convert, without plagiarism, to your use. Try magazines outside your own interests, such as *Pizza News*.

5. Confer with a writer about story ideas that he or she would like to work on. Work hard at being open and noncritical early in the process. Select two or three of the ideas with most potential. Talk about what makes them good.

6. Make a list of outrageous story ideas, ones that, at first glance, will be perceived as impossible to accomplish, completely unworkable, inappropriate for a family newspaper or just plain off-the-wall. Discuss the list with others to test their reactions. How could these "bad" ideas lead to "good" ones?

7. Conduct two brainstorming sessions with a small group of friends. Begin in a very open-ended way: "What stories aren't we doing that we'd really like to get into the paper?" Write down all the ideas. Analyze for yourself people's behavior during the session. Were they positive or negative, supportive or hostile, expansive or narrow-minded? Select one idea from this session and discuss it in a second session. Give yourself only 15 minutes to work on the story idea. See what happens when some collective brainpower is let loose on a single idea.

CHAPTER 9

Coaching for Clarity

Editors who demand good writing get an earful of complaints from frustrated reporters: "Sure, I could write a great story about the Armenian earthquake or the African famine. But disaster ain't my beat. I write about sewers! I write about taxes! I write about budgets! I write about utilities! I write about bond issues! You tell me how I'm supposed to make that readable and interesting!#?!"

This reporter has a right to his rage because he and others like him draw the daily task of writing the toughest stories in the newspaper. No circuses, beauty pageants or oyster-eating contests for these scribes. Only bankruptcies, municipal finance proposals and rate hikes.

But his editor is right too. Good writing should appear in every corner of the paper. Reporters and editors must work together to find new ways to write the newspaper's bread-and-butter stories. Reporters may not be able to write a school board story with the same narrative power that a killer hurricane inspires, but journalists can fulfill their civic responsibilities by making the story clear, comprehensible and readable.

Professor John Robinson of the University of Maryland draws an important distinction between "making information available to the public" and truly "informing the public." Too often, journalists settle for the former. Under pressure of time and space, reporters say subconsciously, "If I understand it, if I get it into the paper without any inaccuracies, then the reader can muddle through it and make whatever sense he or she can out of the story."

William Greider, formerly of the Washington Post, suggests that journalists have a more profound responsibility, one that should affect the way they think and write. Reporters, says Greider, must begin to "have some level of responsibility for what people know and understand."

To meet this challenge, editors must help reporters write in ways that explain important and complex issues to readers. Then informed citizens can make the daily decisions that affect their lives. Should they vote for the councilmember who supported that tax? Should they send their children to public school?

Editors can begin coaching for clarity by applying certain tests to the writer's prose. Is it clear enough so that a reader could pass a quiz on the important information in the story? Is it relevant enough so that a reader could pass along accurate information from the story to another person? If the writer asked the reader, "What's important in this story?," would the reader agree with the reporter and editor?

Journalists who can answer "yes" to these questions are already using the tools of clarity in their work. These techniques help make hard facts easy reading. Writers and supportive editors can both apply them on behalf of the reader.

Envision a General Audience   The writer's sense of audience controls his voice. If the writer imagines an audience of specialists, his language may become technical and convoluted, like this sentence from an editorial entitled "Curb State Mandates":

> To avert the all too common enactment of requirements without regard for their local cost and tax impact, however, the commission recommends that statewide interest should be clearly identified on any proposed mandates, and that states should partially reimburse local governments for some state-imposed mandates and fully for those involving employee compensation, working conditions and pensions.

This sentence assumes an audience of computers or lawyers. The editor must play the role of the reader's friend. These questions might help: "Tell me in your own words what this issue is about." "Can we find a way to simplify this?" "Let's start from the beginning. What exactly is a 'state mandate'?"

Tell It to a Friend   Many readers come to the same story looking for different things. It sometimes helps the writer to imagine she is writing for a single human being, and a familiar one at that. When the writer tells a story to a single person, her voice changes, and her language becomes simpler and more direct.

The editor can often play the role of this friend. One editor asks his writers to write him memos before they try to execute difficult stories. "When they put my name, 'Dear Fred,' at the top of the page, it makes them write in real English rather than that governmental gobbledygook."

Slow Down the Pace of Information   Too much writing on difficult sub-jects is of the "dense-pack" variety: information stuffed into tight, dense paragraphs and conveyed at a rate that takes the reader's breath away:

> The billing structure and data-gathering procedures are geared toward pro-viding cost-based reimbursement to satisfy federal regulations under Medi-care, which insures about 40 percent of Arizona's hospital patients.

Who could pass a comprehension test after reading a story so dense with information? The editor can come to the reader's rescue by getting the writer to slow the flow.

Introduce New Characters or Difficult Concepts One at a Time   A tough story to read, and to edit, introduces 20 characters in a dozen paragraphs. The frustrated reader turns back again and again to keep things straight, or just gives up.

Good editors help reporters introduce one character or one concept at a time. When Chris Welles of the Los Angeles Times told his readers "How accountants helped Orion Pictures launch its financial comeback," he had to explain "generally accepted accounting principles." That done, Welles was able to deal with each of the accounting techniques used at Orion. He introduced them slowly, one at a time. For example, "Certainly the most unusual accounting strategy used by Orion was what is known as 'quasi-reorganization.'"

In such a long, difficult story, Welles gives the reader a chance to relax, to think and to understand.

Recognize the Value of Repetition   Preachers know the value of repeti-tion. They adhere to the old strategy: "Tell them what you're gonna tell them, then tell them, and then tell them what you told them."

Editors tend to be suspicious of repetition. It takes up space. But repeating key information demonstrates its importance to the reader. An editor can recognize the heart of the story and reinforce it in a headline, a pullout quote and a caption.

Bill Blundell of the Wall Street Journal says: "I try to teach reporters that if they have an important point they want to make, make it repetitiously but in different ways. Make it with a figure, make it with an anecdote, and then maybe wrap it up with a quote." Variation saves the repetition from becoming boring and distracting.

Don't Clutter Leads With Confusing Statistics, Technical Information or Bureaucratic Names   The writer and editor must pay special attention to the lead when the story is difficult or complex. If the lead is crammed with information or demonstrates to readers that the subject is beyond their interest and understanding, they will turn elsewhere. Would you read further in this story?

> Efforts to improve housing for Buffalo neighborhoods will receive $5.6 million of the city's 1980–81 federal community development block grant money, according to the application to be submitted to the Common Council tomorrow.

The combination of numbers, bureaucratese and tiresome attribution dooms this lead. The writer could use some coaching from the editor: "How much money is $5.6 million? Who are the key players?" "Explain this application process to me. Is this going to happen or not?"

Use Simple Sentences   Difficult ideas can be expressed in simple sentences. Simple sentences are usually short, clear and easy to read. They contain one clause and one idea. A series of simple sentences also slows the pace for the reader. Each period is a stop sign. The reader has time to digest and assimilate information.

Reporters who forget about their readers write sentences like this one:

> A $3.6 billion compromise budget was agreed to by House and Senate Ways and Means Subcommittees yesterday that pares $1 billion from the previous compromise budget of $4.6 billion, of which $993 million may be restored when it returns to the floor of the Senate next week.

Donald Murray comments, "The more complicated the subject, the more important it is to break the subject down into digestible bites, writing in short paragraphs, short sentences and short words at the points of the greatest complexity when the meaning is too often lost."

A helpful editor sends complicated sentences back to the writer for simplification.

Remember That Numbers Can Be Numbing   Numbers turn off most readers, especially when they are packed into paragraphs or when they bump and collide:

> A proposed elimination of the 2 percent property tax rollback will immediately add $25 to each $1,000 in property taxes paid by middle- and upper-

income taxpayers. In addition, the state is freezing its contribution to the 10 percent property tax rollback, which has been used as a tool to allow homeowners to keep pace with inflated property values.

This paragraph alone is not particularly offensive. But a series of such paragraphs can damage readers' comprehension.

Writers should select only the most important numbers and should explain them in context. Editors can help: "Which number will really tell our readers what's happening?" "That big area of land is just an abstract number. Can we compare it to an area of land our readers will recognize?" "Those big numbers make my head swim. What else costs that much?" "Can we take those numbers out of the story and put them in a graphic?"

Informational graphics are reaching new levels of excellence in American newspapers. The writer's ability to explain complex issues in words and then illustrate them in pictures provides valuable reinforcement for the reader. The clever editor invites the writer into the process. The writer and editor team should watch for important information that might be communicated effectively in a chart, graph or picture.

Translate Jargon   It may take a new city hall writer a month to learn the acronymic alphabet soup of municipal government. Suddenly, she feels comfortable sneaking things like *UDAG* into her stories.

A problem arises when the journalist's language is contaminated by contact with specialists. Unless the journalist translates *capitalization* or *amortization* or *depreciation,* most readers will be left in the dark.

According to page-one editor Glynn Mapes, the Wall Street Journal defines *gross national product* the first time it appears in each story: "the total market value of the output of goods and services in the nation." The Journal's admirable zeal for translating jargon once extended to defining *batting average* in a story about Ted Williams.

Editors learn to read with an "innocent eye," bouncing back acronyms and corporate gibberish.

Look for the Human Side   Writers who write regularly about fiscal policy often fail to escape the clichés of economic writing. Budgets are not human documents, but graphs that look like pizzas. Stories are filled with bottom lines, tightened belts, economic spirals and chopping blocks. These stories seem not to be about people at all. No wonder readers look the other way.

Good writers and editors understand that readers are attracted to human beings in stories. These human beings can be politicians or bureaucrats, or people who are the victims of politicians or bureaucrats.

John Gouch of the Anderson Independent-Mail explains the plight of African-American farmers in South Carolina by focusing on the life and words of a single farmer: "Furman Porter was four years old when he first walked behind a mule plowing up Anderson County's red clay." The story is about the business of farming. The focus on a human being helps readers understand its true significance.

A good editor says, "Show me some people," at least once a day.

Let the Small Represent the Large   It's hard to get a handle on a subject as complex as the "United States bureaucracy" or the "effects of inflation on the American people" or the "economic impact of high technology on the Sun Belt." The key to writing such a story clearly and well is to find a specific, concrete example that represents the larger reality.

"I know there's a problem with vandalism in the county schools," says the editor to the reporter. "But isn't there one school we can focus on to tell the story?" Or "It looks like more top students are starting their college careers at junior colleges. Let's look at all the statistical evidence for that. But let's make sure we identify a student and a family to build the story around."

Consider the Impact   Mike Foley of the St. Petersburg Times teaches his reporters to avoid writing leads that say, in effect, "They held a meeting Tuesday. . . ." The meeting itself is not important, argues Foley. What they did or failed to do is important. Did they increase the millage rate? If so, the writer must communicate the impact to the reader. If necessary, the writer might teach the readers how to compute property taxes based on the new rate.

A city may get a grant to build a plant that will recycle sewage water. The good writer tries to make this news meaningful to the reader: "Next year you may be able to water your lawn, and firefighters may put out fires, with treated sewage water."

Too many stories fail to answer the reader's most challenging question: "So what?" The editor can ask it in the beginning and again and again.

Eliminate Unnecessary Information   The best way to deal with some difficult information is to leave it out of the story. Too many stories contain too much information for readers to digest.

Readers may understand more if reporters give them less. The key to doing this responsibly is to make tough value judgments on the information collected. The result of such selectivity is a more precise, more readable story.

Writers get wed to the material, so immersed in the story that they lose the ability to select the most important information. "I went to the trouble of getting it into my notebook," the writer says to herself, "and by God, it's going into the story." The sharp editor keeps the reporter focused on storytelling rather than on notebook dumping.

Compile Lists   Journalists use a "laundry list" to spell out the most important information in meaningful order. Investigative journalists list their major findings high in the story. A city hall reporter lists the alternatives for financing a new construction project.

Lists create order, or at least the sense of order. They demand that the writer convey information tightly. Lists also create white space and typographical structures that invite the reader's eye to move down the page. Good editors are on the lookout for information in stories that can be transformed into lists.

Cool Off   Killer stories about complex issues often involve intense periods of reporting and learning for the writer. A "cooling off" period helps the writer understand what he knows and how to tell it to the reader. It also gives the writer, with the help of the editor, time to understand what he doesn't know or what he has failed to communicate.

Those who try to publish "in the heat" run serious risks. Some reporters, attempting to explain complicated information, get defensive about long and unclear and complicated sentences. "Of course it's complicated," they tell their editor, "the idea is complicated." That comment masks, "I don't really understand it, so I'll fog over my ignorance with cloudy prose."

Donald Murray recommends that writers "schedule a ritualistic time for standing back" on such stories. "This should be a time when the writer puts all the notes and documents aside, stares out the window, sips a cup of coffee and tries to think what the day's developments mean. It may be a good idea to attempt to put down, in a subject-verb-object sentence, the most important development of the day."

Sometimes a short chat with the editor, preferably on a different subject, cools the smoking writer.

Read It Aloud   If some writers would only listen to their own stories by reading them aloud, they would come to understand how dense and confusing their prose can get. Reading out loud forces writer and editor to experience the linear nature of the reader's path to understanding. One word follows another; one thought follows another. Writer and editor can hear trouble areas even when they can't see them. Many of the best writers testify that they read their work out loud, or at least read it "in-loud," listening to the sounds of their prose in their "inner ear."

When used wisely, these techniques help the writer toward a cleaner and clearer style. Clarity is the journalist's Grail. The quest to achieve it is more than an occupational disposition. It is a form of vision, a way of looking at complex events and issues.

SUMMARY

- Envision a general audience.
- Control the pace of information.
- Introduce characters and concepts one at a time.
- Repeat the most important information.
- Keep the story simple.
- Use numbers selectively.
- Translate jargon.
- Look for the human side.
- Communicate the impact.
- Keep the story short.
- Read the story aloud.

WORKSHOP

1. Read an article from an encyclopedia that attempts to explain a complicated subject. You might look under *E*, for example, and find *Epinephrine, Epigenesis, Epiglottis* and *Epicycle*. Working with a friend, try to explain the concepts, using only what you remember from your reading. Let your friend ask you questions to jog your memory.
2. Study an encyclopedia entry that you found clear. Study the pace of information and language use. Write a brief paragraph describing how the writer made the topic clear.
3. Read some general circulation magazines, such as Reader's Digest and National Geographic. Pay special attention to stories that try to explain complicated issues. Discuss what makes these articles easy to understand. Also discuss ways in which these stories might be improved.
4. Read this morning's paper, and identify an unclear story. Ask a friend to read it, and see if that person agrees with you. Have a conversation about what you don't understand. Make a list of questions you would ask the reporter if you had a chance. Can you rewrite any parts of the story to clarify them, or are there holes in the reporting?
5. Good editors help writers by translating the "heavy cargo" in stories into informational graphics. Examine today's newspaper, looking for examples of material that would be more comprehensible in pictures than in words. Keep a special eye out for complicated numbers.
6. Discuss the difference between "making information available to the public" and "informing the public." As an editor, how could you inspire others to "take responsibility for what readers know and understand about the world?"

CHAPTER 10

Coaching Top to Bottom

Because of inverted-pyramid thinking, journalists devote more attention to tops of stories, especially leads, than to middles or endings. Editors need to help their writers develop techniques that ensure a steady flow from top to bottom for the reader.

Leads

Journalism schools and textbooks make a big deal of leads. Melvin Mencher, a former professor of journalism at Columbia University, calls lead writing "the first, and most important, step in the writing process" and devotes an entire chapter of his textbook, 30 pages, to leads, but not one word to endings.

Many reporters spend too much time crafting the lead, sometimes as much as half their writing time. Often they write leads before organizing the material as a whole, and then wonder why they have trouble making the lead work. And they express surprise when they discover that about 25 percent of their peers seldom write the lead first. Some reporters knock out any old lead to get started, and then come back later and compose a lead that fits the whole story.

Editors can use their news judgment, experience and literary skills to help reporters with leads. Writers' lead-writing abilities will grow with their understanding of writing as a process.

A reporter struggling with leads should think of lead writing as a key part of the process, but not necessarily the first step. Editors should ask reporters to describe, for example, everything they do from the time they finish reporting until they type the first sentence. Except for getting coffee and going to the restroom, the strugglers usually do nothing at all. They just sit down at the terminal and ask, "Well, what's my lead?" A helpful editor can back them up one step in the writing process, suggesting a rehearsal phase, by simply asking, "What's the news?" or "What's your point?"

Let's consider the editor who gets nothing but hard-boiled leads from reporters working out of the trash-compactor school of journalism. The result may read something like this:

> After a debate Tuesday afternoon between Neighborhood Nature Watch and several pressure groups representing various environmental interests in the Largo area, Alfred B. Bronnix, Acting Commissioner for Land Use and Recreation, deferred a rollback of $567,329 in matching funds intended to enhance the $986,397 already appropriated for mangrove restoration by the State Shore Surveillance Committee, according to sources close to Sheriff V. Hugo Taulmy, shortly before his resignation Monday.

Leads that resemble this parody result from the traditional impulse to stick everything in at the top, and from anxiety over reporting complicated stories in constricted space. The editor who wants to inspire change can ask the reporter to read the lead aloud, and then ask what it said. The reporter may fumble and then realize the problem: the reader cannot untangle such sentences, much less remember them. The editor then asks, "What's this story about?" and "Who is the main player?" and "What happens if we put that person's name as the first word in the lead?" And so on.

The opposite problem, sprawling leads, requires a different approach, because reporters tend to admire the writing in their own long leads. What the editor sees as long, they may see as well-crafted. An editor can create the reader's experience for the writer by, once again, reading the masterpiece aloud. The reporter twitches and squirms and blurts out, "This seems long, doesn't it?!" Then the conversation can turn to finding the essence of the piece and crafting that nugget into a shorter lead.

Some stories have no lead at all, just information flowing into more information. Or the lead turns so mushy that the reader misses the transition from lead to the main body. Again, the editor reads aloud, this time asking the reporter to tell her when the lead ends. The writer feels the reader's confusion.

Some stories have multiple leads. Each new paragraph sounds like a lead, and the reader thinks the writer can't decide what the story is about. Editors can help writers identify these multiple leads and can collaborate on choosing the lead that best makes the story's point.

Reporters and editors should be talking about leads all the time. There should be continuing debate and discussion of lead writing, with an eye on finding the best possible beginning for each story in the paper. This list of guidelines should get the discussion started:

1. Remind reporters to keep leads short. Even a very long story can flow from one carefully crafted sentence.
2. Never forget the news. If it is not in the first paragraph, put it in a "nut graph" near the top of the story, and certainly before the story jumps to another page.
3. If a lead is indirect, that is, does not get directly to the point, be sure to include elements that dramatize the news, foreshadow events or create a sense of foreboding or of anticipated surprise.
4. Keep the lead honest. Don't begin with the most startling or sensational anecdote if it is not organically related to the news.
5. Get a good quote high in the story to create a variety of voices and a human focus.
6. Place emphatic words at the beginning and end of the first paragraph.
7. Don't set your standards too high. Every story does not merit a "great lead." But make sure that, at the very least, leads "do no harm" to the reader's understanding of the story.
8. In general, the more important the news, the more reporter and editor should strive for a direct lead.
9. Test the lead out loud to make sure it reveals the tone of the story. If the writer or editor reads the lead aloud to someone else, that person can help judge its effectiveness.
10. When you find a good lead that violates any of these guidelines, use it.

Middles

Many news stories start well, turn into mush after a few paragraphs and end with a neat kicker. The middle of a typical story has no recognizable sequence of ideas, no flow of cause and effect, and no narrative, just puddles of information. This problem has been termed "the disorganized middle syndrome," and editors face it more often than any other problem in coaching.

In longer conferences with editors, reporters often identify their own problems, and disorganized middlers can almost always recognize this one with a little nudging. They complain about writer's block, the inability to find a focus, difficulties with transitions and problems with deadlines. Usually, their accounts of their writing processes lack a step in which they organize their materials.

Editors should keep in mind that many good writers do not pass through formal organizational stages at all. Some people organize their thoughts in their heads on the way back to the office; others think by writing leads. But the ones with problems generally do no organizing at all. They just sit down and bang out a lead.

Once reporters recognize their lack of any organizing phase, they are ready to learn some new tricks for taming their materials:

- Answer Christopher Scanlan's two magic questions: "What's the news here?" "What's my point?"
- Ask what the reader needs to know and in what order.
- Arrange the material into a narrative with a beginning, a middle and an end.
- Write a series of subheads for the sections by visualizing what the story will look like.
- List the players and their motives.
- Think of the middle as a clear path from lead to ending for the reader.
- Ask yourself: "What happened, what caused it to happen and what will happen next?"
- List the most important things, delete half of them and put the rest in an order that helps the reader understand.
- Type two screensful quickly without worrying about sentences or sense, then print it, underline important things and rearrange them into an outline. Then kill the two screensful. (We call this technique "blast drafting.")
- Arrange materials into scenes or chapters or both.
- Explain to an imaginary friend, or even a real one, what you saw and heard.
- Ask yourself: "What do I want to say?"
- Ask yourself: "What happened, then what happened . . . ?"
- Type your best quote and its attribution in one paragraph. Then write a lead and another paragraph to set the quote up and follow it with any necessary context.

All of these methods bring out the most important ideas and concerns. The writer can then write a plan. *Every writer should always write a plan for every story*, in Don Fry's opinion anyway. To keep from scaring writers with the dread "*O* word" (*outline!*), remind them that successful plans can be short, usually four words or so, just a road map of the sections.

Some editors balk at the idea of teaching such basics, especially to seasoned reporters. But teaching saves editing time in the long run.

Endings

Most editors have little experience in coaching endings because reporters tend not to write endings at all. But good storytelling requires a beginning, a middle and an end. Imagine a joke told in the inverted-pyramid form, with the punchline at the beginning, and then a trickle of increasingly trivial detail.

Why should reporters write endings at all? Donald Murray says that the ending "provides the reader with a sense that his or her questions have been answered, reinforces the meaning of the story, provides . . . something worth remembering and stimulates the reader to think."

Endings give the reader a sense of closure and completeness of action, as well as a sense that the writer controls the material by giving it shape. The reader's perception of structure lends authority to the words.

So, why don't reporters write endings? First, many of their teachers taught them not to. Like it or not, the inverted pyramid still serves as the basic template of virtually all journalistic writing, the shape around which most notions of form revolve. Because an ending requires a bit of striking material, writing an ending violates the pyramid's rule that nothing important or attractive should appear at the bottom.

Second, reporters suffer from the "cramming impulse," the compulsion to mash as much detail into the available space as possible. They spent a lot of time and skill and ego collecting the stuff, and they want to squeeze it all in. Because they tend to regard endings as decorative flourishes anyway, they see ending materials as less important than data. So, they leave off the ending to give themselves just one more paragraph for information.

Third, reporters almost universally believe that copy desks chop off endings indiscriminately. Few copy editors will admit to such "Samurai editing." In fact, a number of desk and copy editors say they wish their reporters would write endings. At one paper, the reporters complained that the copy chief did not allow endings, and cut any that crossed her desk. Yet, on any given day, readers could open the paper to find half the stories with true endings. Mythology dies hard.

Editors can encourage reporters to organize their materials with an ending in mind, usually by asking, "What do you want your reader to remember most?" Memory research indicates that whatever comes last persists longest. Depending on the nature of the story, the editor can also suggest some of the traditional ending modes: quotation, projection into the future, note of skepticism or hope, rhetorical question, and so on.

For reporters who do write endings, the most common problems stem from following the traditional movie formula, riding off into the sunset, something like this:

> The Brixckworths gather at the western edge of their feedlot, worrying over their precious acres. How long they stand there depends on the weather, the grasshoppers and Secretary Benson.

This kind of "trailing off" ending invites embroidery and pretty writing. Usually, such endings clash in tone with the rest of the story, and the editor must help the writer discover ways to restore continuity of sound.

Many writers write multiple endings, just as some like to start with several leads. One reporter had trouble making up his mind about the point of his stories; he had the luxury of length and often mashed several stories into one. A typical story for him had four endings. A coach showed him how each ending by itself would change the reader's interpretation of the material that came before. By picking the one ending that made his most important point, he could then cut out extraneous preceding sections.

Here's a trick that works for editors and reporters: cover up the last paragraph and ask if the penultimate paragraph makes a better ending. Then cover the penultimate paragraph and ask the question about the next higher paragraph. This technique usually gets rid of saddling up for the sunset.

Another technique is to ask the writer to compare the ending with the lead. Ideally, the ending reflects the lead somehow, with a repeated word, phrase, image or idea. Often, the ending makes a better lead, and vice versa. When Don Fry pointed out to Roger Simon of the Baltimore Sun that some of his endings and beginnings could be switched, he replied, "Yes, some of them have been switched."

One final technique comforts writers who fear the copy desk and its supposed tendency to slash endings. These writers can identify an alternate target, a paragraph or section that they might prefer to lose rather than their ending. They can indicate for the copy desk the proposed passage with a bracketing pair of notes, such as, "Potential cut begins. . . . Potential cut ends." Some journalists refer to this marking as an "optional trim."

All of these techniques presuppose a coaching environment, an atmosphere in which reporters and editors can discuss, debate, argue and compromise, all on behalf of the reader.

SUMMARY

- Coach leads, middles and endings.
- Help writers conceive the architecture of the story.
- Avoid cramming information into limited space, especially at the top.
- Don't expend all creative energy on the lead.
- Watch for stories that sag in the middle.
- Don't slash arbitrarily from the bottom.
- Attempt to save endings by marking optional trims.

WORKSHOP

1. Begin files in which you clip and save examples of good story leads and endings. Next to each clip, write down exactly what appeals to you about this piece of writing. Force yourself to be specific. Exchange your file with a friend, and discuss your favorites.
2. Confer with a friend before you write the lead of your next story. Try to generate several leads and discuss how each might determine how the reader understands the story.
3. Examine your clips, and select the beginnings and endings that work best. Which are weak, in your opinion? Confer with a friend on how you might strengthen the opening of one story. Write five different leads for it. Discuss with a friend which one works best.
4. Many news stories sag in the middle. Reporters get tired and run out of time. See if you can find a story that has a strong middle, a key anecdote or description that connects the beginning with the end. Exchange a story with a friend, and look for signs of sagging middles.
5. Look at the opening and closing lines of some memorable works of fiction. Discuss the effect of these lines on you and what the author may have been trying to accomplish. Try, for example:

   Charles Dickens, "A Tale of Two Cities"
   Herman Melville, "Moby Dick"
   Mark Twain, "Huckleberry Finn"
   J. D. Salinger, "The Catcher in the Rye"
   F. Scott Fitzgerald, "The Great Gatsby"

6. Survey a group of writers to see what percentage of their writing time is spent on the lead. Also ask them how they "find" their leads. Also ask them whether they can write the rest of the story without writing the lead first. Discuss the results of your poll.

CHAPTER 11

A Vocabulary for Coaching

David Wood, a former writing coach in Minneapolis, observed that writers and editors lack a critical vocabulary for discussing how to improve a story. Listen, for example, to this overheard conversation about a story in which writer and editor sound like a honeymoon couple after a disappointing wedding night:

Writer: Well, what do you think?
Editor: Oh, I don't know.
Writer: What do you mean?
Editor: I'm not sure.
Writer: Did it work for you?
Editor: No, it didn't work for me.
Writer: What can I do to make it better?
Editor: It may be too late.

Such apparently pointless and circular conversations are symptomatic of an important problem in journalism. Reporters and editors have not inherited from literature and tradition a body of knowledge or a critical vocabulary to describe how they work. Poets speak of *alliteration* and *iambic pentameter*. Rhetoricians know *synecdoche* from

Schenectady. Typical journalists have fewer than a dozen useful terms at their fingertips, so few, in fact, that these terms have developed an unnatural importance, creating myopic vision and formulaic thinking and writing. Some journalists never get beyond talking about pyramids, leads, quotes, transitions, kickers and attribution.

The concept of coaching has added many more words, terms that get at the way writers work and readers read. Some have been invented for specific purposes, while others have been borrowed from English composition or creative writing. They do not represent some strange argot, a new orthodoxy to replace an old one. The words most often heard between writers and coaching editors are plain English words describing the processes of writing and editing. They are easy to learn and remember. They allow the reporter to see new ways of writing, and they put writers and editors on the same wavelength.

The following list represents a core of vocabulary for helpful conversation.

Collaborate   Coaching editors want to collaborate, and not just with writers. They sit at the center of a universe in which writers, editors, designers, copy editors and newsroom managers come together. Editors must talk openly about collaboration to create an environment in which good work is encouraged, recognized and rewarded. In such an environment, people team up to meet the needs of the reader. The alternative is the traditional newsroom, where political power plays and protecting one's turf make working together impossible. In an effective newsroom, there is no writing, no reporting, no editing, no photography, no design. There is only journalism.

Collect   Editors know that good writing comes from information rather than from language. If the reporter has not filled the notebook with interesting information, telling anecdotes, revealing quotations and supporting details, he or she will lack the tools to bring the story to life for the reader. That is why the editor and the writer often plan the reporting together, or why the reporter may call the editor from the scene of a story or return to the office for debriefing. The editor may milk the reporter for specific information: "What did the place look like?" or "What made you think she was angry?" The reporter almost always knows more about the story than the editor, but the editor can teach the writer some reporting tricks that will result in better stories. Debriefing helps reporters remember what they know and get it in the story.

Confer   Any meeting between the writer and the editor designed to help the writer and to improve the story can be called a "conference." A conference with a writer on a long project may take an hour or more, but few editors have that much time to devote to a single story. So, the coach shoots for brief conferences designed to move the story and the writer along. A two-minute conversation can help a writer craft a lead. Ninety seconds of conversation about an idea can help the writer plan the reporting. The story conference is the editor's best coaching tool. The best editors have perfected a variety of conference approaches to guide a variety of writers working on a variety of stories.

Details   The search for a good story is often the search for specific, concrete details: the brand of the beer, the name of the dog, the color of the car. John Camp of the St. Paul Pioneer Press calls this "dirt level" reporting. Bill Blundell of the Wall Street Journal preaches the value of "getting down to where the action is." Details create a sense of place and help to define character. Details transport the reader into the story, where the writer can say, "Look at this."

When Gene Roberts of the Philadelphia Inquirer was a young reporter, he learned his craft from a blind editor. Roberts had to read his stories aloud to his editor. "Make me see!" demanded the editor of those reporters who failed to use revealing details. The good editor, role-playing the reader, tunes up the reporter. "What did it look like?" "Help me visualize that." "If you were making a film documentary of that scene, where would you point the camera?" "Was there anything in the room that suggested it was a religious organization?" Such questions sharpen the reporter's senses.

Focus   Perhaps the central step in the writing process, focus gives a story unity and coherence. Most stories should be about one thing. The writer should understand and capture the heart of the story and offer it to the reader. Focus determines what to toss out as well as what to include. Many problems, especially disorganization, result when stories lack focus. Writers and editors search for focus by using a variety of tools: writing the lead, coming up with a headline, making a list of the most important points in the story, and developing a theme or point statement.

Foreshadowing   This technique is well understood in film and fiction, and it has important uses in news and feature writing. In a classic short story, the letter opener placed in the desk drawer early in the plot becomes the murder weapon in the end. In the same way, the reporter can plant narrative details early in the story that will take on full meaning later. Gene Miller of the Miami Herald wrote this lead: "Richard Hornbuckle, auto dealer, golfer, Baptist, came within two feet Friday of driving his yellow Buick Skylark off the Sunshine Skyway Bridge into Tampa Bay." The detail about Hornbuckle's being a Baptist seems extraneous until a description of the man's miraculous escape is followed by a relevant quote: "God, I'm telling you I'll be in church this Sunday morning." In fact, every detail in Miller's lead sentence later appears as part of his story.

If a story reaches a surprising or dramatic climax, the editor can help the writer work backwards: "Without giving it away," the editor asks the reporter, "can we plant a clue high in the story for the reader to follow?"

Ideas   Reporters and coaches are always talking about story ideas. Much of their best work is "front-end" work, conversations early in the process in which stories are conceived, explored, reconceived, rejected and embraced. Editor and reporter press each other to find new approaches to stories, sometimes called "angles," and to hook those new approaches to news elements called "pegs." Coaching editors and reporters believe that the writing process begins at the idea stage. In that sense, editors are idea coaches.

Indirect Lead and Direct Lead   Arguments between writers and editors often concern what should go at the top of the story. A traditional lead, containing the basic news, is often called "direct" or "hard." An opening that describes a person, place or situation, thus delaying the news a bit, is called "indirect" or "soft." When done badly, indirect leads seem self-indulgent and in conflict with the needs of the reader. Some are so shapeless and ineffective they were condemned in an article titled "Jell-O Journalism." Because of that article, some writers and editors comically refer to indirect approaches by the shorthand "Jell-O." Says the writer to the editor: "Do you want me to write it straight, or do you want Jell-O on this one?"

Sometimes editors ask reporters to write two or more leads for a story, and together they decide which one works best.

Nut Graph   Made famous by newspapers such as the Wall Street Journal and the Philadelphia Inquirer, the nut graph is used when the lead is anecdotal or indirect. If the lead begins with a desert scene, the nut graph describes the significance of the scene: it was an important atomic test site in the 1950s. If the lead begins with the description of a funeral, the nut graph offers the basic news value: the dead person is the first woman killed in an underground mine accident. The technique gets its name because the graph contains the "nut" or "hard center" of the story.

Sometimes the nut graph is not a paragraph but a sentence. The nut graph has different names in different towns: the "so-what graph," the "context graph," the "zowee graph," and the "hoo-ha," supposedly mimicking the reader's delight at finding out what the story is really about.

Editors nag writers not to forget the nut, especially in stories with long, indirect leads. The nut graph usually appears as a third or fourth paragraph of a story, and should go before the jump. This little device more than any other, has liberated many reporters from the blandest, most conventional approaches to the news. While occasionally overused, it has earned a place in the newspaper writing hall of fame.

Order   Editors and readers know that the most common problem in newspaper stories is lack of organization. The disorganized writer produces disorganized stories, stories that never reach their potential and are quickly forgotten by readers. Readers like order in stories and remember a story better if they can perceive its overall structure. Good stories have a shape: a pyramid, an hourglass, a circle, a stack of blocks, a loop. An easy way for editors to begin conversations with writers about structure is to ask questions about beginnings (or leads), middles and ends.

Pace   Editors try to help writers control the pace of the story for effect. Writers want readers to advance steadily through a story and to comprehend the information they discover there. Sentence length and word choice help determine the speed and ease of reading. A well-organized long sentence picks up the pace for the reader. A series of short sentences, each period a stop sign, slows the reader down. The more complicated and difficult the material, the slower the pace should be. Too often, reporters cram information into dense, impenetrable paragraphs. Easing a reader into the story is often the solution.

Point Statement   This technique is used to help reporters find the focus of their story. The reporter writes a point statement to answer questions such as "What's the one thing I want my reader to remember?" or "What's the underlying idea of the story?" Don Fry uses his point statement to test all the information he has at his disposal. "If it doesn't help make my point, I throw it out," he says. The point statement may or may not appear in the story.

Here are some examples of point statements: "There are few real cowboys left in an era of cowboy hype." "Jewelry work in Rhode Island is life at the bottom of industrial America." "The council is really frustrated with the developers of the Vinoy Hotel and are ready to take drastic action, including condemnation." The point statement is sometimes called a "thesis" or "theme statement." You should be able to write it in one sentence, or at most on one index card.

Points of Emphasis   Many reporters hide good writing and important information in their stories. A key word, a chilling fact, a startling anecdote, a revealing quote gets lost in a story if the writer fails to place the information at points of emphasis. The key points of emphasis occur at the beginning and at the end of sentences, paragraphs and stories. When placed in the middle, important elements get surrounded by weaker information and sometimes lose their punch. Editors try to help writers to find the best information they have and to move it into emphatic locations.

Points of Entry   This term describes the places where readers are inclined to begin reading a story: obviously, headline, photo and cutline, and lead. But a hundred readers may read the newspaper in a hundred different ways. Those readers benefit from additional points of entry, perhaps a graphic, a summary, a pullout quote, or a well-crafted subhead. Such devices increase the chances that a scanner will derive some information from the story or will become immersed in it from the inside out.

Crafty editors and writers work together to create multiple points of entry. They serve the reader by planning a logical place for the jump and finding enticing language for the subhead.

Rehearse   We think of writing as a motor skill: the writer isn't truly working until his or her hands are moving. Yet, much writing activity takes place in the head. Although they imagine themselves to be procrastinating, many reporters begin writing stories in their heads, while they report, in the car on the way back to the office, in the cafeteria, in the shower. Efficient use of rehearsal time helps the writer write quickly when fingers finally hit keys. The coaching editor helps the reporter to plan and rehearse a story by asking good questions, especially early in the process. With such help, writers gain confidence in their ability to work quickly under pressure, and something negative (procrastination) becomes something positive (rehearsal).

Rewards   Writers and editors seek ways to reward the faithful reader. They organize a story around "high points" that engage the reader in special ways. Such rewards include quotations, anecdotes, descriptions, dialogue, perhaps a bit of humor. The reward says to the reader, "Thank you for reading that last paragraph. It may have seemed a bit boring, but the information was important. So, reader, this next bit's for you."

One reason to write a good and memorable ending is to thank the reader for making it all the way through the story. It's also an invitation for the reader to "come back next time."

This way of writing goes against a bad habit many journalists have: packing all the good stuff into the first three paragraphs and make the rest of the story the dumping ground for the toxic waste in their notebooks.

The reader needs "gold coins" scattered throughout the story. When she finds one, she'll keep on reading to see if there's another. Gold coins might include good quotes, a sharp character or anecdote, or even a surprising turn of phrase.

Rhythm   Writers and editors often use musical metaphors to describe good writing. "Make it sing!" is a favorite editorial imperative, or perhaps a writer at the keyboard will be described as "sitting at the organ." Trouble comes when writers write with their ears, listening for the iambic cadences of the language, and turn the story in to editors who edit with their eyes and thumbs. Such an editor is said to have a "tin ear." One trick is for writers and editors to read to one another out loud, both their own work and that of others.

Scaffolding   When a writer has trouble getting into a story, the editor may say: "Just write me a quick memo about what you saw out there today." The reporter comes back with something like this: "Dear Harry: I only saw one important thing out at the dump site. Two workmen, looking for automobile parts, discovered canisters of illegal pesticides."

The editor suggests that the writer remove the "scaffolding," the salutation and the first sentence, and begin the story with something like the "Two workmen" sentence. In other words, sometimes the writer must write her way into a story, creating sentences that can't appear in the final version but do get the writer where she wants to go. So, the writer erects a scaffold to build the story, but dismantles it to let the story show through.

Select   Good writers use only a small percentage of the information they collect. In that sense, the story is like an iceberg, with the visible part supported by the weight of massive research and evidence.

Too often, writers fall in love with their material and in an effort to squeeze it all in, make bad decisions about what should go into the story. Donald Murray says that brevity in a story comes from "selection and not compression." So, the coaching editor must constantly ask the writer: "What's your best stuff?" or "I know all three quotes are good, but which one is the best?" Editors often miss the opportunity to turn a good story into a great one by not being tougher on writers during the selection process.

Self-edit   Throughout the process, but especially near the end, writers study their own stories, looking to make changes. Depending on the writer, this procedure varies from reconceiving the story, to moving large chunks of information around, to cutting out needless words, to perfecting the language, to correcting spelling.

Some writers foolishly leave the process of revision to others, when, in the best environment, it should be a collaborative process. Editors should try to figure out how much time a writer typically spends on self-editing. Too many writers don't leave themselves enough or any time for revision. Mistakes of haste can be misinterpreted as mistakes of ignorance.

Show, Don't Tell   In kindergarten, future writers and editors played "show and tell." When they get into newsrooms, the game becomes one of "show, don't tell." This ancient writing maxim reminds the writer to recreate evidence for the reader. In describing a character in a story, don't tell the reader, "She was an enthusiastic businesswoman." Instead, show the reader, perhaps in an anecdote, how the businesswoman sold her product to a new client. The editor is always asking the writer "How did she do that?" or "Give me an example of what made you think of her as. . . ." Those questions will echo in the reporter's head when he goes out on the next story.

Voice   When editors and writers use the word *voice*, they may be talking about two different things. Voice is an element of syntax that describes the relationship of subjects and verbs. Preference for the active voice over the passive is so well-established that writers and editors often discuss it when revising stories.

A very different use of the word describes a common illusion in reading and writing. Writers often talk about "finding their voice." Readers and editors may talk about how a story "sounds." All are describing the same phenomenon: the illusion that a single writer is talking directly to a single reader from the page. This effect derives from the natural relationship between the writer's speech and prose, and from artifice and rhetorical invention. All writing, even news writing, has a voice, although the voice may be described as objective, dispassionate or neutral.

Writer and editor can go a long way together thinking about all of these words and the techniques and attitudes they represent. Such words are necessary because they define and describe. Without them, writers and editors cannot see or fully comprehend the strategies and ways of thinking they depend upon so heavily. But there is nothing sacred or special about these words. You can add your own favorites or delete ones you find unwieldy, or even better, create new ones to describe original ways of seeing, thinking, reporting and writing.

WORKSHOP

1. Make a list of your most dependable writing techniques. Even if they are defined in this chapter, write a brief description of how *you* use each and the effect it tends to have on readers.
2. Read some newspapers and magazines with this list of techniques before you. Try to identify at least one example of each technique. Exchange examples with your friends, and talk about your favorites.
3. Interview writers about their favorite writing tricks. Make a list of the tricks that are not mentioned in this chapter.
4. Is there a writing strategy you use consistently but don't know what to call? Discuss it with friends to see if they have a name for it. If not, try to find an appropriate name and share the name and technique with others.
5. Keep a "writing tricks" journal. Paste in passages that display certain tricks, and comment upon their effect on the reader. Use this journal to experiment with writing strategies you'd be nervous to see in print. See if you can gain the confidence to share some of your experiments with others.
6. Read a book about a different kind of writing than what you practice: screen writing, children's literature, poetry, fiction, and so on. See if you can distill some strategies that might work in a journalistic context.
7. Take a passage from one of your recent stories in which you "tell" the reader something. What would you need in your notebook to "show" the reader?
8. What details might turn these "tellings" to "showings"?:
    a. The freeway was crowded.
    b. The pit bull frightened the neighbors.
    c. The mayor is disorganized.

CHAPTER 12

Coaching for Revision

When writers and editors share a common critical vocabulary, they can talk about stories in more careful and specific ways. Such talk leads to revisions that improve the story and help the reader. In this case, Roy Clark talks about his coaching relationship with feature writer Jeff Klinkenberg of the St. Petersburg Times. He reveals how a brief conversation about a story led to dramatic improvements in the piece, all because of the use of a single critical term: *scaffolding*.

Two Writers Talking

Jeff Klinkenberg and I both arrived at the St. Petersburg Times in 1977, Jeff as an award-winning outdoors writer, and I as a neophyte writing coach. We shared an interest in good writing, our children, raw oysters and rock music, so over the next decade we became fast friends. He would share story ideas with me and on occasion show me a draft of a piece he was working on. He came to trust my opinion but never deferred to it. The story was always Jeff's story, and if he made a change based on our conversation, it was always his change.

One of our most memorable encounters involved a personal column
he wrote for a weekly feature in the Times called "Private Lives." This popular spot invites staff writers and free-lancers to explore their personal
experiences and craft stories that connect writers' lives with the news. I
had written three of these columns myself, so I knew the requirements of
the form.

I did no front-end coaching with Jeff on this piece; I merely responded
to his draft, which was pretty far along:

> People tell me I'm a nervous parent. I guess they're right. My daugh-
> ter, 14, wants to walk to a friend's house. "But it's dark," I say. "He only lives
> three houses down," she says. "Why can't he walk over here?" I say. "Oh,
> dad," she says. "Nothing is going to happen."
>
> I am always afraid something is going to happen. Whenever I hear a
> tire squeal, and I don't know where my children are, I look to see if their
> bicycles are safely in the garage. When somebody in a car hot rods down
> the street, I go outside and shout at them to slow down. My father used to
> do that, too, and I was always embarrassed, but now that I have children,
> I can't help myself.
>
> One time a kid on a motorcycle, who had been racing around the
> neighborhood for hours, took a nasty spill when he hit the gravel at the
> corner. No bones were broken, but he was pretty scraped up, and I yelled
> at him to drive sensibly the same moment I was helping him up.
>
> I tell my 7-year-old not to run in the house. She is sure to trip and hit
> her head on the sharp corner of the coffee table. I don't want my 11-year-
> old son to go fishing with a friend down at Little Bayou unless he is wear-
> ing a life preserver and is watched by the other boy's grandfather.
>
> "Don't worry, dad," he says.
>
> When I was young, I did stupid, crazy things that could have gotten
> me killed or arrested. When a train was coming, I'd run out on the tracks,
> carefully arrange my coins on a rail, then jump off at the last second, mak-
> ing sure to be far enough away not to be hit but close enough to see what
> happened to my pennies when they were flattened.
>
> I climbed tall trees to the top. Once, while playing in a treehouse
> made with rotten lumber, a board gave way, and I fell 20 feet into a
> rosebush. The rosebush broke my fall but almost cut off a toe.
>
> I liked to climb on the roof at night and throw water balloons at
> passing cars, and when that lost its thrill I threw guavas, a tropical fruit
> common in Miami. One night, a couple of teen-agers whose car I smashed
> with a guava chased a friend and me for a half mile, over fences, through
> bushes, through back yards where dogs snapped at our heels. We escaped.
> One night, a friend and I built a dummy and, hiding behind a bush,
> threw it in front of a passing car. It screeched to a stop, and an elder-
> ly man got out, shaking, certain he had killed somebody. I am still
> ashamed.
>
> By the time I reached 14 I was a fishing fanatic. I fished for snook, a
> gamefish, in a canal that passed through a golf course in Miami Shores.

I had to trespass to fish, but I was good at climbing high fences, and I didn't mind running from the cops when they were called by golf course employees. The cops would take you to the police station, call your parents and confiscate your tackle. They never caught me.

Sometimes I wish I had been caught. If I had, maybe things would have turned out differently. Maybe I would have stayed away from the golf course once and for all. Maybe the tragedy wouldn't have happened. Keith would still be alive, and on those nights when I lie awake in a cold sweat I would no longer hear him screaming for his mother.

I went back last week. In Miami for business, I had a couple of hours to kill and drove to the golf course. I walked along the first fairway, crossed a footbridge that spanned the canal, passed under the railroad tressle — and then stopped when I saw the dam.

I was staring at the dam when a golf course ranger drove up in his cart. "What are you doing?" he asked. I told him I'd come back to the scene of a tragedy that has haunted me for 23 years. "I remember it," he said. "I lived across the street from the 16th fairway. I remember all the excitement. It was awful."

"I was there," I said.

"Kids still sneak on the golf course to fish," he said. "I chased 10 away already this afternoon."

"Take it from me," I said, "It's no place to fish."

I walked along the 11th fairway to the dam and looked at the sign hanging from the fence.

"Danger," it said. "Automatic Gates Open Without Warning."

I introduced Keith and Kent to fishing. They were 14-year-old fraternal twins I met in ninth grade. Kent was tall, thin and, like me, a nerd who didn't know how to dress and blushed whenever a girl approached. Keith was short and built like a bulldog, with big bones and a neck about as wide as his shoulders. When we played football, he always wanted to play tackle instead of touch. Nobody could bring him down.

It was a Sunday morning. My parents went to Mass. I met Keith and Kent at the golf course fence, and we climbed over. It was March, a little early for snook, but we wanted to try anyway.

Kent did his casting from shore just beneath the 12th tee. Keith and I stood together on a little walkway at the middle of the dam. From there, you could cast under the dam and reach the spot where water and minnows trickled in from the other side.

Keith threw his yellow Creek Chub Darter under the dam. It got snagged on the floodgate on the other side. Keith cussed and said, "I'm going to unsnag my lure." It was the last thing he said to me.

I continued casting. Keith climbed over a guardrail, to the other side of the dam, and lay on the floodgate while he tried to unsnag his hooks. There should have been nothing to it: Just lean in, get your lure and get out.

This has happened to me only once, but on that day I experienced a powerful premonition that something was going to go wrong. The premonition was like a roaring in my ears. I should have shouted, Keith, Kent, look out, but they would have laughed, and so I didn't.

The tide must have reached its highest point for the floodgate to open at the precise moment a teen-age boy chose to unsnag his lure. As the machinery rumbled to life and gears began turning, Keith screamed. Actually, it was a shriek. His upper body was trapped between the floodgate opening and the floor of the dam. Keith knew he was going to die. I'll tell you what he said, though it doesn't mean much unless you can imagine how he screamed.

"Mommy, mommy, mommy. I don't want to die. Oh, God, I don't want to die."

Kent and I jumped the railing and pulled on his legs, which were kicking, but we couldn't pull him out. Pretty soon his legs stopped moving.

It's a Thursday night, almost 8 o'clock, and my 14-year-old daughter says she wants to go to Bryan's house to play cards. We have our usual argument, but this time she wins. "Okay, walk over," I say. "But call me as soon as you get there. Let the phone ring twice and then hang up. I'll know you're all right."

I read the paper and wait. The phone rings twice. She's safe.

I get up and turn on The Bill Cosby Show.

I was fascinated by this story. As a friend, I knew a little bit about this incident from casual conversation over the years, but I had no sense of how horrible it was, and what lasting effect it had had. I told Jeff over the phone how powerful the story was and how much I looked forward to a conference about it. I usually make a few marks on a piece of copy as I read it to remind me of things I want to tell the writer, but I can't recall touching the copy in this case, partly because I had two clear responses to the piece.

Our conferences are usually side by side or over the phone, but late one afternoon I found myself (out of shape) pedaling my bike next to Jeff as he jogged around a nearby park. Conversation turned to his story.

"I want to give you one clear reaction to the piece, and I want to ask you one question."

"Okay, go ahead."

"I think the best, most gripping part of this story is the account of the death of your friend and the childhood activities that lead up to it. Don't get me wrong, I was interested in the part that describes what a nervous parent you were, because I'm one too. But I really got into it from the point you start talking about all the stupid and crazy things you did. From that point on the narrative just builds and builds to this dreadful, amazing conclusion. The beginning and ending are an interesting frame for the piece, but you might think of it as scaffolding. If you take it down, the narrative will have even more power."

This, by the way, is not my usual mode of response. I'm more inclined to begin with questions and lead to some conclusions or observations, but I felt strongly enough about the piece to voice my opinion directly and early. The story was still in Jeff's control. He could embrace or ignore my point of view.

After we chatted briefly about revisions in the story, I asked him my question:

"What happened next, after his legs stopped moving?"

Jeff told me how two doctors on the golf course rushed to the scene and pronounced the boy dead, how Jeff raced home on his bike in desperate search for his parents, and how he wound up on his knees in fruitless prayer.

I usually agree with the maxim "end the story as early as possible," but in this case I found those final details so gripping and emotionally powerful that I encouraged him to use them in the story. I couldn't get out of my mind the image of the boy on the bike racing home knowing his friend was dead.

I didn't talk to Jeff again about the story until I saw his revisions in the newspaper.

Private Lives

By Jeff Klinkenberg

When I was young, growing up in Miami, I did stupid, crazy things that could have gotten me arrested or killed. When a train was coming, I'd run out on the tracks, carefully arrange my coins on a rail, then jump off at the last second, making sure to be far enough away not to be hit but close enough to see what happened to my pennies when they were flattened.

I liked to climb to the roof at night and throw water balloons at passing cars, and when that lost its novelty I hurled guavas, a common tropical fruit. One night, a couple of teen-agers whose car I smashed with a guava chased a friend and me over fences, through bushes and into back yards where dogs snapped at our heels. We somehow escaped.

One night, a friend and I built a dummy and, hiding behind a bush, threw it in front of a passing car. The car screeched to a stop, and an elderly man got out, shaking, certain he had killed somebody. I am still ashamed.

By the time I was 14, I was a fishing fanatic. I fished for snook in a canal that passed through a golf course in Miami Shores. I had to trespass to fish, but I was good at climbing high fences, and I didn't mind running from the cops. The cops would take you to the police station, call your parents and confiscate your tackle. They never caught me.

Sometimes I wish I had been caught. If I had, maybe I would have stayed away from the golf course once and for all. Maybe Keith still would be alive, and on those nights when I lie awake in a cold sweat I would no longer hear him screaming for his mother.

I went back last week. In Miami for business, I had a couple of hours to kill and drove to the golf course. I walked along the first fairway, crossed a bridge that spanned the canal, passed under the railroad trestle — and then stopped when I saw the dam.

I was staring at the dam when a golf course ranger drove up in an electric cart. "What are you doing?" he asked. I told him I'd come back to the scene of a tragedy that has haunted me for 23 years, a tragedy my mind continually dredges up whenever I am depressed or I start worrying about the safety of my own sweet children. Death is no abstraction to me. That a lot of people live to old age is, I know, a matter of luck, of being in the right place at the right time. I am afraid to trust happiness.

"I remember it," the golf course ranger said. "I lived across the street from the 16th fairway. I remember all the excitement. It was awful."

"I was there," I said.

"Kids still sneak on the golf course to fish," he said. "I chased 10 away already this afternoon."

"Take it from me," I said. "It's no place to fish."

I walked along the 11th fairway and looked at the sign hanging from the fence at the dam.

"Danger," it said. "Automatic Gates Open Without Warning."

I introduced the twins, Keith and Kent, to fishing. We were 14 and in ninth grade. Kent was tall, thin and, like me, a nerd who didn't know how to dress and blushed whenever a girl approached. Keith was short and built like a bulldog, with big bones and a neck about as wide as his shoulders. He got into a lot of fights at school, and when we played football, he always wanted to play tackle instead of touch. Nobody could bring him down.

It was a Sunday morning. My parents were at Mass. I met Keith and Kent at the golf course fence, and we climbed over. It was March, a little early for snook, but we wanted to try anyway.

Kent did his casting from shore; Keith and I stood together on a little walkway at the front of the dam. From there, you could cast under the dam and reach the spot where water and minnows trickled in from the other side.

Keith threw his yellow Creek Chub Darter lure under the dam. It got snagged on the floodgate, the mechanism that opens and closes to regulate the flow of water. Keith cussed and said, "I'm going to unsnag my lure." It was the last thing he said to me.

While I continued casting, Keith climbed over a guardrail to the other side of the dam. He lay on the floodgate and reached inside to recover his lure. There should have been nothing to it: Just lean in, get your lure, get out.

The tide, at that moment, must have reached its highest point. Suddenly, the dam roared to life. Gears turned, machinery rumbled and the floodgates began opening. That was when Keith screamed.

Actually, it was a shriek. I still don't know how this happened, and I don't know if I can adequately explain it to you, but what happened was his upper body somehow got pinched between the floodgate and the rest of the dam. He could go neither forward nor back. As the gate came up to allow water to flow from below, life was squeezed from his body. I'll tell you what he said, though it doesn't mean as much unless you can imagine how he shrieked.

"Mommy, mommy, mommy. I don't want to die. Oh, God, I don't want to die."

Kent and I leaped the railing and tugged on his legs, which were kicking, but we couldn't haul him out. Pretty soon his legs stopped kicking.

Kent sprinted to the clubhouse a half mile away for help. I stood crying at the dam, until two doctors, playing golf, ran over to see what happened. One reached into the dam and took Keith's pulse. "He's gone," he said.

A doctor told me to go home; there was nothing I could do. At that moment I wanted nothing more than to go home and cry in my parents' arms. I pitched my tackle over the fence, jumped on my bike and pedaled home as fast as I could, my lungs almost bursting with effort. In my front yard, I jumped off the bicycle while it was still rolling, and ran into the house screaming for my mom and dad. They were still at Mass. I went into their bedroom, fell to my knees and prayed loudly for a miracle I knew was not going to happen.

Keith, my friend, a boy my age, was dead.

Nothing would bring him back ever.

Some observations on this case:

1. The conference about the story was done without a copy of the draft in front of us.
2. Significant changes in the story resulted from a single observation and a single question from the coach.
3. All revisions in the piece were undertaken by the writer, who kept control of the story throughout the process.
4. The story was made shorter, 1,129 words became 993, by building on the strengths of the story rather than dumping on weaknesses.

The story appealed to a wide and diverse audience of readers. One elementary school teacher even read it aloud to her class as a cautionary tale of why children should not take wild risks.

Jeff recalled our conversation about the story and his subsequent revisions: "It was a story I wanted to write, but I didn't really want to write it. I could never have gotten into it by starting with the tragedy of Keith's death. I needed to give myself a reason to do it, which is how I came up with the stuff about being a nervous parent."

What inspired Jeff's revisions was the concept of scaffolding, which I had learned from Donald Murray and Christopher Scanlan. "When we had our talk," said Jeff, "and you mentioned the word *scaffolding*, I knew that you were hitting on something true about the story; I knew it was right."

SUMMARY

- Scaffolding, or writing bits not intended for publication, keeps the writer moving.
- Conferences can happen outside the paper.
- Helpful suggestions delivered directly are part of coaching.
- Occasionally, coach without a text in front of you.
- Develop strengths first, and weaknesses may simply go away.
- Ask the question "What happened next?"

CHAPTER 13

Coaching in Broadcast

Almost every technique for coaching print journalists applies to broadcast journalists as well. Broadcast newsrooms can be fertile grounds that provide special opportunities for coaching. Early in the morning, assignment editors can begin conversations with reporters to help them conceive powerful stories. During the day, reporters consult closely with photographers, discovering ways to visualize stories and to take advantage of natural sound. Brief conferences with news directors or show producers can help the reporter to find a focus for the story that will communicate the news most effectively to viewers.

Valerie Hyman, a prize-winning television reporter, has become a pioneer in the coaching of broadcast reporters. As director of The Poynter Institute's program in broadcast journalism, she teaches newsroom managers how to change the direction of their careers through the process of coaching. Any journalist interested in coaching should heed her advice on how to get started:

> I'll never forget my first coaching experience. It taught me more than any I've had since. And at the time it happened, I wasn't even aware the word *coaching* could apply to journalism!

The corporate news chief at my station took me on the road to visit some of the other stations in our group. He wanted me to work with the most promising reporters so they, in turn, could set even better examples for their colleagues. I sat down to my first coaching session with a young reporter at a small station on the West Coast. He eagerly popped his tape into the machine and proceeded to show me the worst collection of television journalism I'd ever seen.

As it progressed, I struggled silently about what to say when it ended; I knew I didn't want to demoralize him. On the other hand, I couldn't find *anything* good on that tape. The stories lacked focus, his writing was stilted, he failed to match picture and sound, his delivery was sing-song and boring (completely unlike his natural speaking manner), and there was not even one original thought or observation on the entire tape.

By the time the last story ended, I was in panic, literally: my heart was pounding, and so was my head. What in the world was I going to say? A beat passed, and suddenly I heard myself squawking, "Well, if you had the chance to do those stories again, what would you do differently?" To this day, I don't know where that question came from. He responded with great agitation, "Oh God, that was awful! I didn't realize how bad that work was." And he proceeded to lament all the things that were wrong with the stories, even expanding on the lengthy list that had formed in my head as I watched.

It was a revelation. I have silently thanked that reporter dozens of times in coaching sessions with scores of other journalists in the years since. He taught me to keep my mouth mainly shut and my ears and eyes completely open, to ask non-judgmental, open-ended questions, and to praise insight into one's own work. Later, I also learned to find something, anything, to compliment in every coaching session, and always to end on a positive, constructive note.

Thanks to that reporter, and the many I have worked with since, here's my step-by-step guide on how to begin:

1. Start by asking the reporter: "What do you hope to get out of this session? What are your expectations? What would you like to discuss?"

As the coach, you may not know how this journalist has been prepared for this session by a manager or peer. Sometimes the answers you receive are quite surprising and allow you an opportunity you would not otherwise have to straighten out crooked thinking about what is about to happen.

2. Then I ask questions like these: "What are the best features of your reporting, your strengths? What makes you think so? In what areas would you like to improve? Why?"

Discussing these questions may take up the rest of the session, and that's great. After all, one of your main goals is to get insight into journalists' thinking about their own work. For example, often they'll name something as a strength, and later say that's the very thing they want to improve.

If you have another agenda, for example, if the journalists' manager has asked you to work on certain things with the reporters, do your best to weave that into what the reporter says is her or his own agenda. Then they will feel more "ownership" of the session and the course of their development than they would if you flatly stated what the manager wants them to improve.

3. Probe, but ask only open-ended, non-judgmental questions, questions that do not reveal your point of view, and questions that cannot be answered with "yes" or "no," or by making a choice. Some examples:

Open-ended: What was your thinking when you asked the manager that question?
Closed: Don't you think you revealed your own bias in the way you worded your question?

Open-ended: Looking back on that interview, what different questions could you have asked?
Closed: Do you think it would have been better to ask him how he made his site choice or whether his facility is a warehouse?

Non-judgmental: When you sit down to write, how do you consider the structure of the story?
Judgmental: Don't you think the story would have been more powerful if you had used more natural sound?

Non-judgmental: How do you decide whom to call for interviews once you decide what your story is for the day?
Judgmental: Do you look for interviews with people who are emotionally involved in the story of the day?

By the way, this interview technique serves reporters well in their day-to-day work, because open-ended, non-judgmental questions tend to stimulate the richest, most specific responses. You may decide to let the reporter in on your questioning method at this point, and directly suggest it as a way to conduct her or his own interviews.

4. Make sure your body language, that is, facial expression, posture, arms, legs, do not reveal your opinions and reactions. As with the nature of your questions, even if they're positive, your opinions and reactions may tend to stifle the reporter's responses.

5. As you near the end of the coaching session, ask the reporter for reactions: "How do you feel about how this went? How did the actual session compare with what you expected? What will you take away from this session? Let's generate a list of specific things you can start doing tomorrow to apply what we discussed."

This is a good time for you to review with the reporter what he or she wanted to talk about when the session began. If you didn't get to everything on the list, you can come up with a plan of attack together.

I'm still working on how to coach well, and the feedback I get from these closing questions and strategy planning is most helpful.

6. Always, always end on an up-beat, positive note. Talk about what you've learned from the conversation, that you value the reporter's ideas and perspective, or perhaps that you are impressed by her or his insight.

As you get started on this coaching jag, be aware that many reporters' first and last question will be "What do you really think of my work?" I try to avoid answering that question, especially in the beginning of a session. But if they ask it again at the end, I take that opportunity to praise what they do well, and in the absence of that, praise their willingness to improve their work. Almost without exception, praise of some kind is what they need to hear, and they leave satisfied. This is not deceptive or manipulative. It is honest and appropriate.

7. I use the same guiding principles when I write follow-up memos after face-to-face coaching sessions.

I begin my memo by restating the reporter's answers to my first questions in our face-to-face session: "What would you like to get out of this meeting? What are your strong points? What would you like to do better?" I then can easily praise his or her insight and interest in improving, and perhaps move from there to a compliment about a specific aspect of his or her work.

Next, I review the high points of our face-to-face session, making specific references to the stories we viewed together and adding anything else I've thought about since. I try to be as concrete as possible, rather than conceptual. Always, and I mean always, I close on a positive note.

I take extensive notes during coaching sessions, including many verbatim quotes. This is invaluable in writing follow-up memos and in discovering trends in my own questions and the reporters' responses. I think taking notes makes the reporters feel somewhat important and special, as they quickly realize I'm really concerned with what they say.

For me, the payoff for following these general coaching guidelines has been enormous. I have learned to interact with other professionals in a warm, supportive way. I now use non-judgmental, open-ended questions more often in my personal life, thus avoiding what might otherwise have been adversarial incidents. And best of all, I have discovered that I can be a good human being and a strong, constructive professional at the same time. May you enjoy the same benefits from your work.

SUMMARY

- Ask about expectations.
- Ask about strengths and weaknesses.
- Ask open-ended, non-judgmental questions.
- Control your body language.
- Ask for feedback.
- End with praise.
- Follow up with a memo.

PART FOUR

Working Together

CHAPTER 14

A Climate for Coaching

Coaching can succeed in any newsroom climate, but certain climates work better than others. Ideally, a newsroom would encourage good and even great work by ordinary reporters. Journalists need to feel that their superiors and peers recognize, encourage and reward good work. Good editors celebrate good work, often with very simple techniques.

Bulletin Boards

Many newsrooms have bulletin boards, with contents ranging from simple announcements to bloodbaths. In one newsroom Don Fry visited, the ombudsman proudly displayed "his" bulletin board. Fry asked why the board had a heavy, hinged plexiglass cover and a sturdy padlock, and the ombudsman replied that "reporters tend to vandalize it." Guess what was on the board that needed so much protection: virulent complaint letters from readers, accompanied by copies of the ombudsman's groveling replies, which always blamed the reporters.

Bulletin boards serve best when they become "Good Work Boards." The board becomes a place to celebrate fine work and, more important, to stimulate conversation about what constitutes good work. Reporters and editors gather around new items and debate what works and what needs work. Like a good newspaper, a good bulletin board provides a daily agenda for professional conversation.

Here are some items that might appear on such a board to celebrate good work and to stimulate discussion:

- Terrific clips from the previous day's paper
- Positive comments and suggestions on those clips
- Clips from other papers with commentary
- Articles and lists and tips about good writing
- Compliments from higher managers and other media
- Notices of contests
- Responses to all of the above

And here are some items that do not belong on such a board, because they tend to discourage helpful discussion:

- Blasts from readers and managers
- Stylebook nagging
- Guild nagging
- Cheap shots in any form
- Promotional material
- Pictures too awful to print in the paper
- Routine announcements

Thoughtfully controlled, a bulletin board becomes a device to set forth models of good work. Reporters respond primarily to two positive things in a newsroom: praise and story play. Good story play is, of course, a form of praise, and the best story play is posting the piece in a place of honor.

Commentary on such items gives the coaching editor a chance to specify what's praiseworthy, getting beyond such simple comments as "good story," although "good story" gets better results than silence. A helpful comment might run like this: "I like this lead because it hooks the reader with the graphic description of the little girl and tells the reader that the story will focus on her, not on the unidentified motorist who hit her." Or "Great headline. It makes the straight lead jump. Well done, Joe." Or "I love this anecdote, especially the way it catches the superintendent's embarrassment over the banner misspelling his own name."

Commentary can also suggest other and/or better ways to do something praiseworthy: "This lead gets the city engineer on stage quickly, but it might read better if we held his full title until a graph or two later." Or "Super kicker on this story, makes the reader feel Springsteen's powerful presence. But the two graphs above it have a sense of closing too, perhaps confusing the reader with multiple endings." Or "Great quote in the third graph, but notice how every story on this page has a quote in the third graph. Have we fallen into a formula?" Notice how the praise precedes the suggestions.

Reporters being guerrilla warriors, such bulletin boards will attract a certain amount of skeptical response, usually scrawled across things, such as "Says you, I think this lead sucks!" Nasty notes from supervisors have a way of sneaking onto the boards. Coaching editors need to monitor the board carefully and frequently, removing anything that might undermine their messages. A wise coach might have clean copies ready to replace anything that gets vandalized.

Bulletin boards work best when reporters see them as a forum open to everyone. Any member of the newsroom should feel free to contribute to a Good Works Board. But the coaching editor needs to check it frequently to remove any nasty messages.

Newsletters

Many coaches and coaching editors publish in-house newsletters as a tool for improving writing. We traditionally call such newsletters Winners and Sinners, after the famous New York Times critique. Unfortunately, most newsletters become huge lists of vile sins, with only a token winner thrown in now and then. Why? Because sinners are easier to spot, easier to write about, and more fun.

All the remarks about Good Work Boards would apply to newsletters. The best ones, such as Paula La Rocque's FYI at the (Dallas) Morning News, induce conversation among writers. These newsletters include stories worthy of praise, tips and hints, reprinted articles on writing and a little bit of nagging.

A good newsletter can reflect the views of one person, the editor or coach who produces it, or of the whole newsroom. Ideally, the newsletter becomes a forum reflecting differing views of writing and style. A newsletter will fail if reporters see it as an extra weapon that editors use against them.

Courtesy helps. Take the bylines off stories that get criticized, and underline them on stories praised.

Contests

Many editors have a healthy skepticism about contests because they can create coziness with industries that award prizes, cause jealousies in the newsroom and produce reporting stunts. Despite these hazards, contests can give coaching editors a way of celebrating great work. Internal contests work best because coaches can tailor them to obtain desired results.

The newsroom must see the judging as fair and not political. Well, not too political. Where managers do all the judging, reporters tend to see contests as manipulative. Managers also tend to spread prizes around among departments: "Say, sports hasn't won in months, so let's. . . . "

If juries contain editors, they shouldn't contain many, and certainly not a majority. To ensure fairness and freshness, some newspapers use a jury of previous winners, who rotate onto and off the board.

Prizes vary from a pat on the back to writing opportunities, to cash. USA Today at one time used the cover story as a prize for writing excellent stories. Unfortunately, that method sent mixed signals: the prize for writing short was the opportunity to write long! Some newspapers give up to $50 for each month's winning story, and some use merchandise prizes or free dinners. At the Providence Journal-Bulletin, the winner gets to write an essay on the reporting and writing of the winning piece. Every few years, the paper prints these essays in a book titled "How I Wrote the Story." The prize for writing well is writing more!

Reporters will say (cynically) that the only prize that counts is cash. But the most effective prize in terms of improving writing involves peer recognition and discussion of techniques and standards. So, the coaching editor needs to design a contest that seems fair and gives prizes to stories and efforts the coach wants prized.

Writers Groups

Writers groups encourage discussion among reporters on writing, and a good group can support the coaching editor's efforts. To start a writers group, you need only three things: two writers and a clip. At the opposite extreme, you could have a complex organization with formal workshops, support sessions and visiting experts. The simplest ones seem to work best, and the most complex ones usually start small.

A writers group talks about news reporting and writing. Many meet over lunch with no formal organization beyond naming someone to pick a subject for discussion and take care of scheduling.

Many groups begin as vehicles for obtaining feedback from peers. Pat Murkland of the Riverside (Cal.) Press-Enterprise finds editors more oriented toward getting out the next paper than discussing previous stories. So, she hands out samples of her writing for others in her group to discuss.

Depending on the tone of the newsroom and the cast of characters, talk can take on a negative or a positive tone. Discussion succeeds best when the members choose constructive criticism, with a heavy emphasis on strengths rather than weaknesses. The traditional slashing style of newspaper critiques may prove too severe for a writers group. Such traditional bloodletting is counterproductive in any group, any format, anywhere.

Participants should also focus on larger issues and techniques rather than quibbling about format. Anyone bringing a stylebook into a writers group deserves hisses and boos.

Some groups prefer to study materials from outside their own newspaper, to avoid ridiculing each other and to keep up with what's going on elsewhere in the profession. Members bring in clips from stories they liked or disliked. The Poynter Institute's "Best Newspaper Writing" series provides good source material for this type of discussion, because the reprinted stories come packaged with study questions, interviews with the prize-winning authors and bibliographies.

Writers groups can also focus on techniques rather than on individual stories. Reporters might invite newsroom experts to share their procedures and secrets. The best telephone interviewers on the staff might explain and demonstrate tricks, and answer questions. The best notetaker in the city room could show others her notebook on a complicated story and explain how to get the quotations right. At the Lakeland (Fla.) Ledger, a business writer showed how to find business angles in community stories.

Reporters seem most interested in the following topics, which should provide enough fuel to get any group started:

- Handling quotations and attribution
- Lead writing
- Tricks for faster writing
- Interviewing techniques
- Sourcing
- Developing story ideas
- Alternatives to the inverted pyramid
- Organizing time and materials

A year's worth of topics appears at the end of this chapter.

The group might ask reporters who write striking pieces to discuss how they found the story, or how they solved key problems. A writers group might want to work its way through Christopher Scanlan's excellent anthology, "How I Wrote the Story."

Some groups invite speakers from inside the paper, from other local papers or from other media. Sometimes police or business leaders will come and explain their needs and special concerns. Few local speakers need compensation beyond a free lunch, if that. The group might offer to swap speakers with other groups outside the paper.

One topic quickly kills a writers group: bitching about management. Reporters do that all the time anyway, and doing it in a more organized way becomes tedious. The group might agree in advance to exclude grousing and gossip.

The simplest groups require little organization, but complicated ones may require full logistic support. Either type will need some photocopying, someone to handle scheduling and simple publicity, and someone to pick topics and materials. More organized groups might want to appoint formal leaders, not only of the organization but also for the discussions. Ambitious groups could recruit the newsroom's intellectual leaders. Any group needs at least two people to run it to handle conflicts with scheduling, illness, and so on.

Most groups meet in the daytime, preferably during lunch. Holding night meetings might put a strain on family and social life. A writers group at the St. Petersburg Times supposedly failed because no one had enough energy left to meet at night.

Management plays various roles in these groups, everything from total and deliberate exclusion to handling the entire show. Reporters thinking about forming a group that excludes management should touch base with managers to disarm any fears of an incipient guild or an informal pressure group.

The best groups get started by reporters who want to talk to each other about reporting and writing. The problem is usually how to take the first step. The answer: just ask who's interested.

Writers groups never last forever. They tend to peak in about six months and need occasional revving up, or even refounding. Because of the heavy demands on their time and attention, journalists drift in their less formal commitments.

How do you know when your writers group is really working? Here are some signs:

- Writers start asking each other for help with stories.
- Writers chat about good writing instead of about bad editing.
- Editors get jealous of all the fun their writers are having, and form an editors group.

Reporter Coaches

Some reporters make better coaches than editors do, probably because reporters see each other more or less as equals. The "boss-ism" of editors can get in the way.

Reporters already know the basic techniques of coaching, because coaching skills are essentially reporting skills: asking good questions and

A Great Experiment in Newswriting

Journalists suffer from the inertia of habit. The production problems of creating a newspaper each day seduce journalists into
assembly-line mentalities. Taking safe approaches to stories, thinking
conventionally, avoiding risk, doing what you did yesterday become
the paths of least resistance. But they lead to mediocrity.

The great journalists have a special vision and see another way.
They seek to energize writers and redefine news. In the words of
television reporter Robbie Gordon, they see each new story as a
workshop in which they discover something new about their craft
and the world.

In 1973, Chuck Hauser joined the Providence Journal-Bulletin as
executive editor after a bitter strike had demoralized the paper. He
overcame suspicions about his leadership style and encouraged a
more aggressive approach to writing and reporting. To change the
writing environment in the paper, he enlisted the help of Joel
Rawson, whose unconventional approach to newswriting inspired
one of the great little revolutions in American journalism. Bruce
DeSilva, who worked at the Journal during this grand experiment,
tells the story:

About two years after Hauser arrived in Providence, he gave Rawson,
then thirty years old, one of the biggest jobs on the paper, putting him in
charge of the Sunday Journal. "Till then," Hauser says, "Sunday was just
another day of the week. It could have been Tuesday, with more space. The
Sunday paper should be special. I thought Joel was the most exciting and
creative editor we had."

Rawson and Hauser met with six promising reporters to talk about
writing for the Sunday paper. A reporter named Ron Winslow, now a page-
one editor at The Wall Street Journal, brought up an accidental drowing he
had covered. What he couldn't get out of his mind, he said, was the two skate
marks leading up to the hole in the ice. "Why didn't you put that in the
lead?" Rawson asked. "Because," Winslow said, "the paper wouldn't print hard
news stories written like that." "Yes, we would," Hauser piped up. It was
official. The paper wanted something different from the traditional, just-the-
facts-ma'am news story.

Rawson and the six reporters met every Wednesday. They talked about
how to write the news differently, better. Rawson had them read chapters in
books by Joan Didion, Ernest Hemingway, and Bruce Catton because he
couldn't find newspaper stories of the kind he envisioned.

Then came the February day that Thomas E. Hone, Jr., a University of Rhode Island honors student, mowed down three people in a wild automobile ride that ended with his own death at the Jamestown Bridge. Bruce D. Butterfield, now a business writer for the Boston Globe, wrote about it using an outline Rawson had scrawled at one of the Wednesday meetings. The result was the dramatic tale of four people moving inevitably to their deaths. If George Potter had not stopped to chat with his brother, if Debra Westbrook had walked a little faster, they would not have been in the way when the car careened down the road.

"Rawson had found a way to tell the news as a story, using dramatic devices borrowed from the theater and the novel," says Andy Burkhardt, then a copy editor and now the state editor. "And television. He was very much a child of television. He wanted to make the readers *see* the news."

"Guys like myself," Rawson says, "were the first part of the TV generation to rise to the point that we could have an impact on newspapers. The people we were working for, and then began to supplant, did not acknowledge T.V. At the Journal, we were trying in our own way to capture a share of your day. And then that tube lights up, and it is in color, and it moves, and it talks, and it has background music. Newspapers had to change whether they wanted to or not."

"Rawson had fire, a knife in his teeth," says Mark Patinkin, one of the paper's columnists. "Once, in a dispute about a story, he literally leaped over two desks to get at me. He really cared about the story, really cared about your stuff. You knew he was on your side even when he was yelling at you."

With Rawson teaching, threatening, and cheering from desktops, more and more writers caught on. Suddenly, the Journal-Bulletin was one of a handful of newspapers expanding the definition of news and finding better ways to write it. It became known, among journalists, as "a writer's paper."

Christopher Scanlan, a former Journal-Bulletin reporter who now covers Washington for the Knight-Ridder newspaper chain says, "Rawson wanted extraordinary reporting about the lives of ordinary people, not just celebrities, but people who were usually ignored by newspapers. Once he asked me to go shopping with an old person and then write what it was like to buy soup when you've only got $3.15 in your pocket. It turned out to be a story about what it was like to be old and alone; it wasn't about shopping at all."

Soon, there was a remarkable story in the paper nearly every Sunday. Winslow made readers smell the smoke and feel the terror as 54 young women fought for their lives on the burning fourth floor of Providence College's Aquinas Hall. Barbara Carton donned welder's leathers and struck an arc so she could tell readers what it was like to "burn wire" at

Electric Boat. Irene Wielawski put readers at the side of a terrified intern trying to stick an intravenous line in a dying baby's arm on her first day as a doctor. Butterfield and Scanlan let readers watch a security guard gun down an intruder in a Warwick church. And then they showed readers the same guard sitting in the church a few days later, a Bible in his lap and his gun still on his hip, with the chalked outline of the body near his feet. This was news written with the color and drama of fiction. But it was more than news. Many of these stories touched hearts; they said something about life.

We can draw a few lessons from this experiment:

- Habit and insecurity make papers dull.
- Leaders inspire change by action.
- Small but active groups can transform the whole paper.
- The best advertisement for better writing is good writing well played.
- Extraordinary reporting makes the ordinary extraordinary.

listening to the answers. The best reporters practice "soft interviewing," that is, asking friendly questions and listening intently to build a relation of trust with the interview subject.

In fact, reporters may have to unlearn some things to become coaches. The following reporter practices hurt coaching:

- Saying, "It sucks"
- Showing cynicism and making cutting remarks
- Bashing editors
- Focusing on small negatives and magnifying them
- Overlooking strengths
- Acting out of impatience and haste

Above all, reporter-coaches have to suppress their competitive urges and the impulse to take over the story.

Reporter-coaches may have more time for other reporters than editors do. Many editors attend too many meetings, which gives them little time for training their writers. Reporters can coach each other in two-minute bursts, or over lunch or a beer.

In an ideal newsroom, everyone, reporters and editors, would coach. The problem might be chaos of advice. Coaching editors need to foster agreement on basic principles of writing and style, "what the paper wants."

This collegial consensus needs careful fashioning and tending. Having a series of meetings to discuss good writing may get reporters and editors on the same wavelength.

Unfortunately, no one has yet managed to get any group of journalists to agree on what constitutes a "good story." Confronted with a fine clip, journalists will tend to "tear it apart" by focusing on one detail after another. They tend to elevate their style preferences into universal rules. Some serious journalists (and teachers) seem to equate starting a sentence with the word *but* as a violation of the structure of the human mind.

Some questions produce consensus faster than others:

- What constitutes "deep reporting?"
- What kinds of leads are appropriate for different types of stories?
- Which stories recently published in this newspaper could we call "model" but not "perfect" stories?
- Does this staff prefer bright stories or traditionally flat ones? Really?
- Whom should we imagine as our readers? Watch out for cynicism and condescension here.

Some newspapers have used a buddy system to train new reporters and upgrade the skills of others. Joel Rawson of the Providence Journal-Bulletin calls its system the "lead dog/sturdy dog" approach. The sturdy new reporter goes out on stories with the veteran reporter, who "shows the kid the ropes." They write stories together, and the veteran teaches the beginner his or her best reporting and writing strategies.

Finally, why should reporters want to coach other reporters? Because everyone in the newsroom will perform better when writing becomes easier and faster and more appreciated. Coaching is a form of teaching, and teaching is the fastest way to learn things. Everyone would learn together and collaborate.

Copy Desk Visibility

We could write a tragedy about the modern copy desk. Copy editors remain second-class citizens in the newsroom and the butt of reporters' humor and scorn. Reporters call copy editors "trolls," "mad slashers," "people-haters," "librarianish" and the dismissive "they": "Look what *they* did to my story."

But copy editors keep the paper clean, accurate, explanatory and consistent in usage. They catch errors that reporters miss in their haste and absorption. Reporters need to know and appreciate them. *No program to improve newswriting will succeed unless it includes the copy editors.*

Copy desks can undo experimental writing by regarding it as non-standard and editing it back into traditional forms. They can crush the life out of freedom by wielding a heavy stylebook. They can dull bright writing by making it "safe."

Coaching editors must bring copy editors into the conversation. They can even teach copy editors to coach reporters and each other. Editors can promote conversation with the copy desk at all stages of the writing process, but most important, at the beginning.

All these devices will assist the coaching editor in creating a climate that recognizes, encourages and rewards good work. But they remain the background. The foreground is talking with writers one-on-one.

Topics for a Writers Group

1. Cleaning up quotations
2. Attribution: when, where and how much
3. Writing leads "that sing"
4. Writing endings that might survive the copy desk
5. Smooth transitions that don't lose the reader
6. Writing a one-hour story in 20 minutes
7. How to get and give feedback on stories
8. Special problems in dealing with victims and families
9. Developing good relations with copy editors
10. How to get interviews with inaccessible people
11. Interviewing techniques for difficult sources
12. Anonymous sources and the problems they cause
13. How to find 10 good story ideas a week
14. Story shapes other than the inverted pyramid
15. Organization tricks for busy reporters
16. How to cover meetings without falling asleep
17. Special problems in reporting AIDS stories
18. What to do (and not to do) in a hostage situation
19. Legal and ethical aspects of privacy
20. Avoiding biased language and stereotypes
21. Using techniques borrowed from fiction in newswriting
22. Freedom of Information update
23. Representing ethnic communities and minority groups fairly
24. Using features techniques in hard news stories
25. Telephone interviewing as a fine art
26. What photographers can teach writers, and vice versa
27. Who reads this newspaper anyway?
28. Writing clear sentences and paragraphs
29. Using numbers in stories without losing the reader

30. How writers can think graphically
31. How to coach and get coached
32. Freebies and conflict of interest
33. How we won the X prize, and how to win it again
34. Suggesting headlines and subheads to the copy desk
35. How to avoid plagiarism, accidental and deliberate
36. Punctuation: a powerful writing tool
37. Explanation and context in news stories
38. Should reporters lie or disguise themselves?
39. Public records refresher
40. Keeping up with the changing American language
41. Strategies for quick revision
42. Brightening up stories
43. Roundtable: my best writing trick
44. Techniques for effective description
45. Techniques to improve notetaking
46. Dealing with burnout
47. Preventing and overcoming writer's block
48. What *accurate* means in newswriting
49. Brainstorming techniques to improve reporting
50. What makes a good news story good?

SUMMARY

- Bulletin boards can celebrate good work and spark discussion.
- Newsletters work if they stay positive and encourage discussion.
- Contests need to be simple, honest and aligned with writing goals.
- Writers groups inspire reporters to help each other.
- Writers groups should not gossip or complain, too much anyway.
- Reporters make good coaches because they don't outrank people they coach.
- The copy desk should attend all discussions of writing and editing.

CHAPTER 15

Talking to
Each Other

After 10 months, Justin's first newspaper decided to
fire him because, among other deficiencies, he couldn't
spell. Yet he had graduated from college in mass com-
munications, earned a masters degree in a distinguished
international studies program and won a fellowship
in newswriting and editing at The Poynter Institute. His
teachers remembered this reserved young man as a solid
reporter, a wry observer and a witty writer. What had
gone wrong?

Several of his editors had expressed their disappoint-
ment with Justin's performance to Don Fry, one of Justin's
teachers at Poynter. Fry assumed they were telling Justin
the same things, and therefore never told him about their
remarks. When Fry met Justin's assigning editor at a seminar, he learned that the paper might possibly fire Justin
that summer. So Fry offered a deal: if the paper would
send him back to Florida and cover his expenses, Fry
would coach him for two weeks on his own time. One condition: Justin had to volunteer.

Shortly afterwards, the managing editor called. They
had run the young reporter through a harsh review
and put him on eight-weeks probation. Then they pro-

posed Fry's offer to him, and he accepted. The editor listed Justin's deficiencies:

- Weak reporting and no progress in reporting skills
- Inability to engage subjects
- Failure to understand what constitutes a good story
- Flat writing
- Poor grammar and spelling
- Failure to compare copy with the printed story
- Failure to reflect on editors' questions
- Poor communication with editors

What a devastating list, the negative of every skill expected in a reporter!

The managing editor thought perhaps Justin had chosen the wrong profession, and he expected the coaching to fail. Fry asked if Justin had any hint of these negative opinions before the review. The editor thought not, indeed believed that Justin did not even understand the seriousness of probation. Fry asked if they had helped him with his reporting and writing, and the editor replied, "People who seek help, get help." Fry thought to himself that this reserved young man would not likely ask for help if he had no idea he needed it. Most editors forget that reporters tend to interpret a lack of feedback as a sign of approval.

Fry looked up the evaluation he had written about Justin as a student: "Solid reporter and organizer. Needs work on sentence clarity and organization. Person of strong character and integrity. Understands the meaning of fairness and objectivity. Needs a nurturing editor." That last remark reminded the teacher of his advice to the editor who hired him: lacking experience, Justin would need guidance in the newsroom.

How could a bright, ambitious young reporter forget everything he had once learned? The St. Petersburg Times had printed a story on the homeless he wrote as a student, yet now he couldn't succeed in a paper one-tenth the size, with a well-deserved reputation as one of the best small dailies in the United States.

When Justin arrived in Florida, Fry compared his clips with raw copy. To his astonishment, Justin's editors proved absolutely right. They had to rewrite everything he submitted. Mistakes in spelling and grammar blighted his copy. His pieces lacked human interest and voices, and had no structure whatever.

Talking with him, Fry learned that neither his editors nor his colleagues had given him any warning of an unfavorable review, no clue that the editors disliked his work. As Justin put it, "Everybody knew except me."

Experienced coaches know that answers to problems lie in process, not in copy. So, Fry decided to examine all Justin's work habits and all his preliminary materials as he developed a local piece assigned on a subject Fry knew well, the Salvador Dali Museum in St. Petersburg.

Justin barely made his deadline, and his 58-line story had four misspelled names, 23 other misspellings, and 26 grammar or format errors. His lead and kicker, printed here verbatim, seemed both flat and flabby at the same time:

> For one hour a week, Griselda Boler becomes the artisctic translator for Salvador Dali. . . .
>
> Tour sizes vary from onl a handful of people at a time to large fgroups of 4–050 people who eagerly follow the guides around as they explain the hidden features in Dali's works that line the musuem walls.

The errors seemed more careless than ignorant, the sentences more unrevised than incompetent.

Fry remembers vividly the moment when he first spotted the vital clue. He spread the raw materials for Justin's Dali story on his desk: scribbles, computer jottings, pieces of drafts and a notebook. He mumbled to himself: "Hmmm, he takes many of his notes in nearly complete sentences. These sentences have no grammatical errors. These sentences have no misspelled words. Abbreviations yes, but no misspelled words. How can he write good sentences in his notebook and make so many errors in his copy? Aha! He doesn't have problems with grammar or spelling; he has problems with *speed*."

Fry examined every step in Justin's writing process, diagnosing bad habits that slowed him down, sharpening organizational skills to speed him up. And the first step in Justin's organizing phase was a killer. He would write a page in his notebook like this:

As attendants
people entered
the cement
steps of the
BF Center
organizers
readied their
tables for
petion drives
supporting
the stadium
3 large
tables cover
with fresh
white

Back in the office, he might type that page and the following pages into one solid block, something like this:

```
asattendantspeopleenteredtheceme
ntstepsofthebfcenterorganizersre
adiedtheirtablesforpetiondrivess
upportingthestadium3largetablesc
overwithfreshwhitetableclothsone
tableofferedvisorsandstickers8wo
rkersthegreenlabelsandsimpleGOpe
oplebeganarrivingshortlyaft4came
tovoicesupportforstsofarbehindfo
rwarduntilstandingstillalotignor
anttowhat'sgoingdon'trealizewhat
'sgoingon [etc.].
```

He explained that he liked to split the computer screen horizontally, putting his notes in one half and composing on the other half. He typed tight blocks so he could see more information on the screen at once. He had difficulty finding things he needed in such a mass of gray and sometimes could not tell where a quotation began or ended. The teacher suggested that Justin weed the notes as he typed them into readable lines.

Justin spent an inordinate amount of time organizing his materials and usually ended up with a disorganized mess anyway. He simply had no idea what he wanted to say before he began to write. So, the teacher reviewed the tricks of story planning. Fry explained how to put codes in the margins of notes so Justin could recover vital facts and quotations quickly. He taught Justin the ruthless discarding of wonderful but irrelevant stuff. He suggested that Justin answer two key questions: "What's the news here, and what's my point for my reader?" And especially, he drummed into Justin the necessity of writing from a simple plan.

Justin had also fallen into the trap of trying to craft a "perfect lead" first. But the story often changed as he wrote it, and the lead would no longer fit. They discussed how to skip the lead or write any old lead and then come back later to write one that matched the final version of the story. Justin learned how to draft at high speed and revise carefully.

Justin had never allowed time for proofreading, since he barely made his deadlines anyway. If he had time, he ran the copy through a computerized spelling checker before turning it in. He was astonished to learn that spelling checkers do not really check spelling, but merely tell whether the words in the text match the words in the computer's memory. For instance, a spelling checker will find nothing wrong with this sentence: "Their is know weigh too fined thee read shoos" ("There is no way to find the red shoes"). Every item in that passage equals an English word, so the computer endorses the spelling.

To experience how sloppy copy can overload the copy desk, Justin timed himself while he corrected 10 errors in his text. He was amazed to discover how each correction can cost an editor 10 seconds, not to mention the irritation.

His stories lacked convincing human voices. Because he wrote slowly, he had little time to find good subjects, much less to interview them well. He did bring back quotations, but they sounded more like data than speech. As he gained time for reporting, he learned how to put real human beings at the top of the story, saying real things, with real objects surrounding them to reveal their characters.

In two weeks of story assignments and coaching, Justin had cut his planning and writing time by half, and later by two-thirds. He gained time to find good subjects and to interview them in depth. He reserved time for proofreading and turned in nearly perfect copy.

At the end of the second week, he wrote a finely honed profile of a local business leader, full of telling detail and revealing quotations, with a real scoop on plans for a bellwether business. The piece began this way: "Watson L. Haynes came into work smiling Wednesday. Haynes, the owner of the Business Service Center, located at 249 Central Ave., had been debating whether to give up a downtown retail location and move his business to Tampa." The (St. Petersburg) Evening Independent printed this piece, and Justin returned to his newspaper with a major clip in his pocket.

A week later, Justin's editor called Fry and expressed his amazement at Justin's new speed, ability to capture good subjects, clear organization, high polish and cheerfulness. He mockingly accused Fry of sending back a "ringer." Subsequently, Justin doubled his story output, survived a second probation period and got a new nurturing editor and a raise. He saw his career path open wide before him.

Why did this intelligent and well-trained beginning reporter apparently forget everything he had learned in five years of professional schooling? An unfortunate combination of bad working habits slowed his writing. Slow writing undermined his reporting. Annoyed by his messy copy and low productivity, his editors judged him incompetent, but neglected to help him or even to express displeasure with his work. He tried harder as he became dissatisfied with his own performance, but dug himself in deeper. His frustration blinded him to the basics of reporting and newswriting. Any journalist who has weathered a bad spell will recognize these symptoms of helplessness and despair.

But did Justin need two weeks of coaching in Florida to be redeemed as a journalist? Or did he need attention from his editors? They pronounced him incompetent from his copy alone, without talking to him about his problems or his working habits. Every problem solved by the coach could have been solved in Justin's own newsroom.

But a later talk with Justin's editor revealed how foreign the idea of coaching can seem to a traditional newsroom. The editor told Fry that Fry's coaching showed the editors how they might handle reporters like Justin. They had thought they did not have the skill to do the basic analyses required, and they lacked the time for extended coaching on the desk. But, as the editor put it, "Now we'd take the time to do what you did, because we see it works. These problems can be solved in a newsroom, but you have to know how to do it."

Several months later, Justin's editor told Fry that Justin did write better and produced cleaner copy, but still had serious problems with initiative and motivation. The editor thought that the editors could build on the solid base of Justin's improved reporting and writing, and they might eventually solve the larger problems.

A week later, Fry talked to Justin and asked him if his new editor was helping him with his initiative problems. You guessed it. No one had ever mentioned any problems with his initiative or motivation. Later, Justin asked his desk editor about these problems, who said he had no problems with Justin's initiative or motivation.

So, some editors at Justin's paper still had some doubts about him and his future. His performance gradually sagged again. Finally, Justin, with too many doubts of his own about his future and the ability of his supervisors to communicate with him or each other, left journalism for the Peace Corps.

The first principle of the human side of editing is talking to the person at the next desk. Every day.

SUMMARY

- Talk with reporters who are having problems.
- Talk with reporters who are not having problems.
- Intervene early; don't wait for problems to compound themselves.
- Schedule regular performance evaluations.
- Encourage reporters to come forward to seek help.
- Reporters must ask for feedback, whether they think they need it or not.
- Examine the working methods of reporters, not just final copy.
- Don't be afraid to offer specific, helpful criticism.
- Keep coaching.

WORKSHOP

1. You are Justin's new city editor. Other editors in the department tell you they think Justin is a weak reporter and writer. They offer the list of faults on p. 137. "Has anyone ever talked to him about this?" you ask. With the help of a friend, role-play a conversation between Justin and his editor.

2. Based on your reading of this case study, make a list of recommendations you think would help reform the organization for which Justin worked.

3. A few editors conduct regular performance evaluations of their reporters. In most cases, the evaluation involves both conversation and written exchanges. Identify an editor who conducts such evaluations. Interview him or her about how the process works. Try to interview a reporter who has been so evaluated. How do editor and writer feel about the process?

4. One of the most difficult things in the world is to offer a person negative appraisals. Most of us have worked with or for someone whose behavior we would like to change. With the help of a friend, role-play a conversation with this person. You must play the role of the other person, while your friend offers your perspective.

5. Compose a written performance evaluation of your own work. Begin with things you do well, but do not neglect to deal with areas for improvement.

6. With the help of some friends, make a list of characteristics you would look for in hiring a new reporter. Now make another list of things for which you might fire a reporter. What values are inherent in the two lists?

7. It took an experienced coach to diagnose the deep flaws in Justin's writing process. Or did it? What kinds of things can coaching editors do to help reporters overcome serious problems in their work?

8. Justin looks like an exceptional case. Is he, or is he just a striking example of a common situation?

CHAPTER 16

How to Get Coached

Reporters want to get their best work in the newspaper, but they may distrust or even despise the editors they write for. So, their dealings with editors often turn into guerrilla warfare.

Roy Clark asks reporters, "How do you get your best work into the paper?" Here are some answers from benighted reporters working at unenlightened newspapers:

Never make eye contact with your editor. No matter what you're doing, keep your head down and look busy. If the editor looks your way, pick up the telephone quickly. If you make eye contact, you're doomed to another assignment.

Go editor-shopping. Know the daily schedules and habits of your editors. When the bad one goes to dinner, hand in your story to the nice one.

Turn in your story as late as possible. Some editors will let things slide if they have no time to fix it. Warning: other editors may just chop from the bottom.

Lobby on one thing to hide another. If you put something controversial in your 10th paragraph and you want to save it from editors, put something really out-

143

rageous in the fifth paragraph, negotiate hard to keep that and grudgingly give it up. The real zinger in paragraph 10 will fly right into the paper.

If you get a dumb assignment, stall. Smile at the editor and act friendly, but point to the compost heap of stuff overflowing your desk and seem hazy about when you can get around to it. In 75 percent of the cases, the editor will forget about the story, or it will lose its timeliness, and you won't have to do it at all.

Don't be afraid to go over your editor's head, but do so diplomatically. Lobby for a good assignment with your boss's boss over lunch. Casually sit down and gab about your work and plant some seeds. Next thing you know, a memo will float down from on high to your editor: "Jim, maybe we should send Johnson to spend a week interviewing Lady Di. . . ."

If things are going badly, get your spouse to help. Have your spouse make emotional phone calls to you at work about your late hours. Unfeeling editors might change things for you if they think it will save your marriage. You might get bonus points for children crying in the background.

Lie to your editor. If your editor sends you to ask the mother of 10 dead children for their pictures, don't make a big ethical case out of it in the newsroom and risk your job. Just leave the office for a while and come back with a whopper: "All the photos were destroyed in the fire."

Reporters evolved these guerrilla tactics to cope with the gorilla cage atmosphere of newsrooms. It doesn't have to stay that way.

Writers need advice on the training and cultivation of editors. Such advice can come from editors themselves, especially those who want writers to assume responsibility for their own professional development. No good editor wants reporters feeling unhappy or frustrated in their work. Such people can easily become malcontents who will poison the atmosphere of the newsroom.

An editor can clear the air with a statement like this to the writers: "The editors are supposed to be in charge here, but we're all in this together. Each writer in this newsroom is responsible for making this a better place to work. We need activity rather than passivity. It means you've got to take some risks along the way, to say what's on your mind, and to help make this place more responsive to the needs of our readers."

Then reporters can adopt a whole new series of more helpful strategies, such as the following ones collected from collaborative newsrooms.

Reporters Must Learn to Praise the Kind of Editing They Want The egotism of some writers makes them behave at times like golden retrievers: they want to be petted even after they've chewed the carpet. Writers who need praise and encouragement act hypocritically when they fail to give the same kind of support to their editors. You can't expect editors to welcome you when you only approach them to whine.

When the editing works well, find a way to praise it:

- "Thanks for that catch. Next time, I'll check all of the numbers."
- "Good headline you wrote. I especially like the way you got the focus of the story without stealing the lead."
- "That suggestion about transitions really worked. It allowed me to cut the story without damaging the material."
- "Thanks for sticking up for me on this one. I hear you took some flak at the meeting."
- "Writing the story that way meant some big risks. In retrospect, I'm not sure how well it worked, but thanks for letting me try."

The next step is harder: helping your editor to become a more effective collaborator by pointing out behavior you find destructive to your work. Yes, you've got to be a little brave. Maybe very brave.

All reporters, especially inexperienced ones, have the same recurring nightmare. You have a problem with an editor and want to work it out. Finally, you get up the courage to approach the ogre in his office. The result is always the same: "Get out of my sight, you little ____! Who the hell do you think you are coming in here and telling me how to do my job?! Imagine some college jerk who's been here just two years trying to tell me what to do! Come back in 30 years, kid!"

Well, it could happen, and does. And reporters must be brave enough to speak their minds to editors who are capable of change, and even to some who are not.

The conversations need not be acrimonious. Reporter Berkley Hudson took this tack in response to a negative editor: "Look, I understand what you're saying about the story, but I've got to tell you that every time I hand you a story, all I get is negative criticism. I have some trouble with that. I want you to help make me a better writer, but I want to make you a better editor too."

Some of the following approaches to editors have worked for other reporters:

- *Explaining.* "I like to give you story ideas, but that doesn't mean I want to do them myself. Every time I come to you with an idea, you want the story by Thursday. Sometimes I want to do it, but sometimes I want to give you the idea for some other reporter. If you want more story ideas from me, we've got to work this out."
- *Complaining.* "I'd like to talk about attribution. I know it's important, but sometimes it's more important than other times. I work hard on

my stories, and it's a bit demoralizing to have you stick 'police said' after every third sentence. It's gotten so that the desk will stick in 'police said' even when police didn't say it."

- *Asking for consistency.* "You told me two months ago that I should be trying to get my stories in earlier so there'll be time for better editing. I'm getting my stories in early, but they seem to be just sitting on your desk. If no one is reading them before deadline anyway, why can't I spend two more hours polishing and proofreading?"

Such criticism and suggestions should be made in a good spirit and to improve the system. They will be better received if you have built a reputation as a person who is willing to praise when things go well. If they are received badly, you have important knowledge you can use to make career decisions. Do you really want to work at a newspaper where criticism of editors or of the system is unacceptable?

Most writers respond that their editors are not willing to change, so why rock the boat? But there is one overriding reason why editors do not change: *no one tells them what they're doing wrong.* Editors benefit from coaching, even coaching from below.

Editors May Not Like Surprises   If you're going to try something unconventional, tip editors off early to make them allies rather than obstacles.

Roy Clark remembers the time he got special help from his editor on an unorthodox approach to a story. In 1978, Clark interviewed author Stephen King by telephone. King was promoting a new book and was emerging as the most popular and prolific horror fiction writer of his time.

Clark approached his editor, Dorothy Smiljanich: "Dorothy, I've read four of King's books, and I've got the interview transcribed. Now I want to try out an idea on you."

"What are you thinking about?"

"I think I can write this interview in the form of a short story, a kind of friendly parody of King's style. I'll create a scene in which King's voice comes to me in some kind of nightmarish apparition. But I'll use the obvious fiction to frame real quotes from the interview. I'll show you a sample tomorrow, and if you don't think it works, I can write it conventionally."

Smiljanich approved the idea and after sampling Clark's draft, ordered a special illustration to run with the piece in the Sunday arts section. By bringing his editor into the process early, Clark turned Smiljanich into a strong ally for an offbeat story.

Reporters seldom see the full load of meetings and planning sessions necessary to put out the newspaper. Editors plan packages, allocate space and raise expectations based on promises made to each other. Those promises often derive from early conversations with reporters. So, when a story shifts or the news changes, the reporter must inform the editor.

Steve Lovelady of the Philadelphia Inquirer puts it simply: "If you're going in a new or different direction, send up a flare."

It Helps to Cultivate Positive Relationships with Everyone in the Building We mean secretaries, librarians, photographers, artists and copy clerks. If you act like a jerk, you'll be treated like a jerk.

The best reporters cultivate sources at every level on their beats. The sharp reporter covering the courthouse learns the names of the secretaries, the bailiffs, the clerks working in the records room and maybe even the maintenance person. Really shrewd reporters know the secretaries' children's names, maybe their birthdays. Good information comes from all directions, and courtesy pays off in the form of news tips and quick service. A reporter wants a source to be responsive but, more than that, wants the source to come forward without invitation.

Ironically, when the reporter returns to the newsroom, he may forget all the good habits he uses in the outside world. He snaps at a receptionist, barks orders to a librarian, brushes off his editor and complains out loud about the incompetence of the copy desk. Such a person has declared a cold war against his colleagues, and has wounded himself along the way. Reporting a good story is tough enough without creating enemies who could have been valuable allies.

Roy Clark walked through the newsroom of the Greensboro News & Record with Greta Tilley, an award-winning features writer. "I've never seen anything like it," said Clark. "Everyone in the building knew Greta by name and smiled when she approached. Greta said something personal to each one. She was clearly the object of great respect and affection, so much so that I almost expected flowers to spring up at her feet and little birds to alight on her shoulders. You got the sense that the staff of that paper would do anything to help her."

Reporters Should Get to Know, Socially and Professionally, People on the Copy Desk Volunteer for a brief stint on the desk so you understand the pressures copy editors face. It will make you a better writer and collaborator.

A reporter from a southern newspaper volunteered to spend some evenings on the desk. He worked elbow to elbow with rim editors, observed the dreadful condition of some of the copy, watched the effects of reporters not meeting deadline, and felt the pressures of trying to prepare yards of copy for the next day's newspaper. Over time, he began to socialize with the copy editors, to share meals and an occasional beer.

Coaching Your Editor

One newspaper reporter took it upon herself to help her editor
become better. She engaged him in conversations about the quality
of work and the level of morale in their department. He then invited
her to put her opinions in writing and to include a critique of his
work as editor. The writer composed a long and detailed memo. It
began with praise for the editor followed by a frank discussion of the
case of a writer who, unable to do his best work for this editor, left
the paper. But the heart of the memo was a list of specific suggestions on how the editor could improve his relationships with writers:

1. Spend more time talking to your writers, one on one, in an informal way. Visit *their* desks, and ask how they're doing. "Everything okay
at home? Anything bothering you? What do you think about this or
that? Is this story a difficult one? Easy? Can I help?"

It's public relations, I know, but it's important. Your staff tends to
associate you, unfairly, with punishment, discipline, humiliation,
terse computer messages and so on. You are tough, and serious, but
you are not Count Dracula! You're funny and, as I've found out, extremely
caring. I wish you'd let more people see that side of your personality.

2. Try to find more time to consult with writers on key stories from
the beginning. "What should this story accomplish? What do we
already know, and what do we need to know? Whom should we talk
to?" And after the reporter finishes an interview, have another five-
minute consult. "What did you find out? What's the focus? What's
your lead? How are you going to end this?" Two things happen:
1) you eliminate some deadline bombshells, 2) the writer begins
to look at you as a friend and not someone who will be second-
guessing later.

3. A number of writers (rarely this one) are uneasy when you are
editing their work. By the time you've finished with them and their
stories, they often feel they have failed miserably. "Why didn't you ask
this? This doesn't make sense! This is unfocused!" Such questions/
comments, and the editor's tone, strike at a writer's professionalism
and integrity and are never forgotten. I know it's not your intention
to demoralize, but some very sensitive people are demoralized.

The problem, I think, is this: most writers are never more

vulnerable than when they have turned in a story. Even the good ones are afraid they have failed, lost their talent, forgotten key questions and so on. Sometimes they have, of course. But I don't believe it helps to dwell on the negatives initially. I think it's more important to talk about strengths and build confidence: "You have good quotes in here, and I like this transition. But what about this? I wonder if we could focus this story more if we moved this to a sidebar? And I keep thinking that maybe you should call this guy and ask this question. Maybe I'm dense today, but I don't understand this line. What's it mean?"

Yeah, I know. We're not running a nursery school here. These are professionals, after all, and sometimes the work is so poor you want to scream. But the point is, we have to work with what we've got, to get the best out of them at all times. If we don't, our section is weaker than it should be. A writer absolutely needs to think of an editor as an ally who wants to help make the writer look good. If a writer is afraid the editor is sitting as judge and jury, waiting to pounce, he or she will freeze up.

Result: low productivity.

4. Be generous with praise, even if it sometimes means stretching a bit and talking about just a sentence or a quotation or the way the writer used punctuation. Praise motivates a writer *much more* than fear. When you have been generous with your praise, the writer will be more likely to accept your criticism.

5. I know how busy you are, but I'd love to see you write more, 1) for the pleasure of reading your prose, and 2) for its possible impact on the staff: "If he can write something this good in his spare time while administering one of the paper's busiest departments, maybe I can be more productive, too." Writing would also give you conversation fodder when you visit writers. They'd love to know if the story was hard for you to write, whether you were happy with it, and what you may have done differently if you had more time. Try to establish common ground.

Let more people get to know you. When they do, I think they'll like you as much as I do.

All writers and editors can learn from the tone of this memo. It is direct, honest, supportive and specific. It touches on what the editor should stop doing, what he should keep doing and what he should start doing.

What prevents more communication of this nature from writer to editor? Paranoia, distrust and a fear of reprisals. It takes guts to try to get your boss to change his or her behavior. There may be some anxiety and unpleasantness in the exchange. But at least you are not acting like a helpless victim. It's time for editors to receive performance evaluations from their reporters. Editors will put themselves in the best position to shape the careers of writers only when they give up trying to prove they are in charge.

"There's something I don't understand," said the reporter to the copy editors one evening. "Over on that side of the room, they complain about how you all butcher copy and make big changes in the story without consulting the writer. But you never do that with my work. What's going on?"

"Well," responded a slot editor, "you're not a jerk."

Writers and editors who get to know each other personally develop mutual respect and learn how to help each other solve problems of mutual concern. Meanwhile, at most papers, some reporters may not know the name of a single copy editor. The result is suspicion, acrimony and bad service to the reader.

It May Help to Write Memos, Before and After Certain Stories Have Been Published   A written message to an editor carries a different authority and concern than a conversation. A written proposal for a story idea has a better chance of succeeding, even after that idea was turned down face to face. An editor may still turn down the idea for good reasons, but if you want a fair and careful hearing, it helps to write it down. Such a memo might look like this:

> I'd like to do an education story on the value of teachers' reading literature to students in class aloud. A couple of recent books talk about this, and I plan to read them. But I've recently reread a book that was read aloud to me by my eighth grade teacher. I could add an interesting first-person element if I could read this same book to an eighth grade class. I'd observe the students' responses and interview them and so on. It would probably take an hour a day for about two weeks, which means I could work on daily stories along the way. What do you think?

Typing out a brief post-mortem on a published story also helps, especially if it includes ideas on how to do such a story better in the future.

If You Sit in Your Chair Waiting for Feedback, You'll Sit There for a Long Time So seize the initiative. You have to approach editors, seeking specific criticism on individual stories. If you are not getting any coaching, you've got to ask for some.

But you must not waste your editor's time. Do not turn conferences into psychiatric consultation. If you can't accomplish something in two minutes, or in five minutes on some occasions, you are not being efficient enough. When possible, consult early in the day and hand in stories early enough for meaningful consultation.

Don't be afraid, even in the face of unenlightened editing. Every time you write, a number of editors evaluate your work, from the copy desk up to top management. You've got a right to know what they think in specific terms. And you should not settle for brushoffs, such as "We put it in the paper, didn't we?" or "We'll let you know if anything is wrong."

The work of writers and editors should be evaluated on a regular basis. But the more active the writer is in the process, the more valuable the feedback will be. After all, editors evaluate you behind your back. Why not invite them to speak their minds to your face?

Reporters Must Be Aware of the Political Pressures on Editors Maybe something has been promised at a meeting or has come down from you-know-who. Every once in a while, lay down your resistance to what seems like a dead-end story idea and "do one for the club," in the words of Joel Rawson of the Providence Journal-Bulletin.

A reporter says to the editor, "Hey, I know you're short-handed today. If you need me, I'll be happy to pitch in." That reporter will earn not only the gratitude of editors but also more freedom in the long run. An editor who knows you'll back him or her in a crunch will become a better lobbyist for your work and ideas.

That's why it is important for you to volunteer to help coach writers in the newsroom. Even the talented editor may lack the time and energy to do important coaching. You can help create informal networks of sharing stories and ideas. You can take an inexperienced reporter under your wing.

In short, you can take responsibility for making your newsroom a more humane and creative place in which to work.

SUMMARY

- Praise good editing.
- Make suggestions to editors to help them improve.
- Warn editors about surprises.
- Be nice to people in the office.
- Cultivate the copy desk.
- Write memos to pitch story ideas.
- Seek useful feedback.
- On occasion, "do one for the club."
- Take responsibility for the development of your own career.

WORKSHOP

1. Interview reporters about the "guerrilla warfare" tactics they use in their battle with editors. Analyze these negative strategies and describe the conditions that inspired them.
2. Name the editor who is most helpful to you in your writing. Make a list of the ways in which this person helps you. Based on that list, have a conversation with the editor in which you offer some specific praise. If there is some way in which the editor could become even more helpful, tell him or her in specific terms.
3. Make a list of the people who are the most supportive of your work. Name others who could be more supportive if they got to know you better. Find an opportunity to get to know their names, to introduce yourself to one of these people, and to find some areas of mutual interest.
4. Conceive and explore an unconventional story idea. Now imagine you are pitching it to an editor. With a friend playing the role of editor, offer the story idea in conversation alone. Now write a one-page memo about the story and offer it to another friend/editor. Follow up with a conversation. Discuss any differences in these encounters.
5. Writers are often unaware of the political pressures exerted on assigning editors. Interview an editor about these pressures. What strategies has he or she developed to deal with them?
6. Make yourself a promise that for one week you will seek out as much feedback on your work as possible. Make a short list of people who are in a position to evaluate your work, not just supervisors. Approach these people face to face and ask them specific questions about your work. What did you learn from this process?

CHAPTER 17

Copy Editors
as Partners

An ancient newsroom myth explains how writers at a newspaper improve. It describes the process this way: The writer gets an assignment, undertakes the reporting and drafts the story to the best of his or her ability. The editors then take control of the story. An editor repairs it because there is no time for consultation. If a hole ruins the story, an editor fills it. If a mistake creeps in, an editor corrects it. The process seems clean and efficient, but how does the writer learn?

The myth contends that the writer wakes up in the morning and reads the story carefully, noting all the changes the editors made the night before. Studying these changes will educate the writer. He or she will not repeat his or her mistakes. With no mistakes, he or she will write better.

Even if writers behaved this way, and few do, this method of learning is highly inefficient. The myth suggests that a writer, without the benefit of correspondence or conversation, can read purpose into an editor's revisions.

In fact, many of the people in charge of making last-minute changes in copy, let's call them all "copy editors," never communicate with writers at all. And writers never communicate with them. In some cases, the system does not allow it, as if editors and writers were monks silenced by a vow.

No wonder, then, that reporters and copy editors at many papers see each other as enemies. They even have pet names for one another. Writers who work in the daylight see copy editors as vampires who appear in the newsroom after dark to suck the life's blood out of copy. To the writers, these editors are anonymous moles. They are the "hacks," the "butchers," or simply "Them." One writer always blames his problems on "some copy editor," always anonymous. At a writing and editing workshop, Roy Clark asked the copy editors in the room to raise their hands. When they did, the reporters booed.

How easy, in the face of such abuse, for the copy editors to dismiss writers as whining, egotistical, self-indulgent "prima donnas." After all, many copy editors are writers too. They write headlines, cutlines, summaries and digest items. Don Fry calls them "the most important writers at the paper," because readers tend to be attracted to a story by the headline and cutline rather than the lead, that is, by what the copy editor, not what the reporter, writes.

Many copy editors have practiced the art of coaching each other for years. On good desks, editors are not attached to their computer terminals as if they were life-support systems. They share work with each other, testing out headlines, turning to each other for specialized expertise, critiquing pages on a regular basis, and growing in the craft along the way. All of the strategies of the human side of editing discussed in this book are practiced on the best copy desks.

Most problems occur when the copy desk must confer with the assigning desk or with reporters, especially on last-minute changes in stories. Examine for a moment the language in that last sentence: "when the copy desk must confer with the assigning desk." Our very jargon dehumanizes the process, for desks do not confer with each other. People do.

Many obstacles get in the way of face-to-face consultation. Computer technology, for example, tempts us to replace face-to-facing with interfacing. Anonymous critiques written hastily on the computer in the "notes mode" can reinforce the writer's paranoia that some dark force is looking over his or her shoulder. This paranoia runs the risk of becoming paralysis in the face of new technology that allows editors to "peek" at the work of writers during the drafting process. In the right hands, such tools can be used benignly, offering much needed specific feedback to the writer. But they are inherently dangerous because they lack the nuance of human conversation.

Another obstacle is time, the fact that copy editors are usually overburdened with work during the production process and think they have little time for consultation. Even if they did, the editors have a different rhythm of work from the reporters. When they are gearing up, the reporters are gearing down. When they need an answer to an important question, the reporters may be in bed. Their schedules are as different as their biological clocks.

These normal problems are often exacerbated by bad newsroom management. Perhaps shifts do not overlap enough to create good communication between those who work during the night and those who work during the day. Perhaps the newsroom is organized so that copy desks are isolated, making relationships difficult. Too often, top editors forget to bring key copy editors into a project early enough. The result is that they become blood clots when they could have served as anti-coagulants. And on some papers, copy editors are discouraged from talking with writers. At one paper, copy editors don't have phones on their desks.

These conditions lead to inaccuracy in stories and bad morale in newsrooms.

Something called a "protocol" could lubricate the process for making last-minute changes in copy. The protocol is nothing more than a set of guidelines, a sort of map that shows lines of responsibility and communication. It attempts to describe a process that reporters and editors might follow when faced with last-minute changes in copy. Because these last-minute changes often create friction between the copy desk and other parts of the paper, they run the risk of undercutting a coaching environment.

A protocol is best developed collaboratively, among groups of reporters, assigning editors, and copy editors. At meetings to develop the protocol, various groups describe the process from their points of view. There are inevitably, and should be, friendly arguments and debates, along with the study of individual cases to test the procedure.

On March 16, 1989, a group of copy editors attending a Poynter Institute seminar drafted a statement of purpose for such a protocol:

> Newspapers are in the communication business. Yet, too often, within our own newsroom, the lines of communication break down. Copy editors make last-minute changes without consulting reporters or assigning editors. Reporters and assigning editors fail to make themselves available at critical times. Copy editors, assigning editors, and reporters debate the merits of editing changes with no clear understanding of what process to follow or how to resolve an impasse.
>
> The result has been resentment and a lack of trust among colleagues whose collaboration is essential. Copy editors are frustrated. Reporters feel powerless and demoralized. Occasionally, errors are introduced or deadlines missed. In the end, the quality of the newspaper suffers.

We realize that the news day is inherently unpredictable and that no policy can address the various situations that might arise. Our goal is to formulate flexible guidelines to help resolve these conflicts.

This is more than a set of steps to be followed by the copy desk alone. These guidelines are addressed to the entire news staff so that all will be operating within a common and consistent framework.

The process should function smoothly, with each newsperson having a clear idea of his or her role and the steps to follow in order to produce an accurate, well-written newspaper on deadline.

Our guidelines are flexible, in order to allow for contingencies such as the absence of a key player or severe time constraints. We regard this as the beginning of an effort toward clarifying roles, easing tensions on deadline and creating a climate of cooperation and respect.

This statement introduced a list of 38 typical changes that copy editors are often called upon to make at the last minute. These changes were divided into three categories: consultation required, consultation desirable and consultation not required. There is nothing sacred about the judgments made by the Poynter group. In fact, they invite debate, negotiation and compromise.

Changes in Which Consultation Is Not Required

1. Correcting a misspelled word.
2. Correcting an obviously misspelled name. If the name is odd or tricky, consultation is desirable.
3. Updating news in a story.
4. Making minor cuts for space.
5. Tightening or uncluttering sentences, unless they are obviously important sentences.
6. Correcting most violations of the stylebook. Some violations that accomplish specific purposes may be acceptable.
7. Clarifying the attribution, that is, making clear where certain information comes from.
8. Adding little facts, if they are obvious.
9. Localizing wire copy, unless controversial.
10. Eliminating casually libelous material, but depends upon the complexity of the story. Follow-up consultation is always required when it comes to libel.
11. Removing information from police story that implies conviction.
12. Resolving conflicts between the story and a graphic, photo or cutline, if obvious.

Changes in Which Consultation Is Desirable

13. Filling a hole in the story, but consultation is required for a big hole.
14. Moving a sentence, but consultation is required if an important sentence.
15. Moving a block, but consultation is required if an important block.
16. Revising a problem headline.
17. Deleting obscenity unless crucial to the story.
18. Paraphrasing a quotation.

Changes in Which Consultation Is Required

19. Cutting a story that is less newsworthy than expected.
20. Changing a lead.
21. Revising for fairness.
22. Cleaning up quotations.
23. Changing a controversial fact.
24. Revising the tone of the story.
25. Reconciling inconsistency with past story.
26. Making major cuts.
27. Cutting a story that comes in longer than budgeted, if breaking news made it longer.
28. Editing a problematic photo.
29. Correcting factual or identification errors in cutlines, unless obvious.
30. Dealing with a source who calls in new information.
31. Using anonymous sources against policy.
32. Pointing out conflicts of interest.
33. Holding a story.
34. Punching up a dull story.
35. Doubting a story.
36. Selecting a photo.
37. Cropping a photo.
38. Creating a sidebar.

We do not suggest implementing these guidelines. Rather, we offer them as stimuli for conversation among the players in the newsroom.

To test the system, let's try out a case. It's 1988, and a top political reporter for your paper visits a small town in your circulation area to get a sense of how people are responding to the presidential campaign. The reporter talks to dozens of citizens in many of the town's little meeting places and finds a person to focus on. She is something of a character, a bit odd, but very quotable and surprisingly knowledgeable and concerned about presidential politics.

The writer crafts this lead:

> In the tiny town of Wimbish, Ohio, 51-year-old Martha Rae Fulton is known as a talker. During most seasons, the talk is of the weather or her grand-daughter or her prize-winning rutabagas. But in this presidential season, Mrs. Fulton's gab has taken a decidedly political turn. If you run into her in the grocery store, the beauty shop or the laundromat, she'll probably bend your ear about who should be president.
>
> "Dukakis comes across to me as a kind of heartless sucker," she says in a voice made husky by years of smoking, "but old Georgie boy is a wimp, pure and simple. Now what kind of a choice is that?"

The story cruises through the editing process, and just about everyone who reads it likes it. The writer and assigning editor agree on a few changes, and it is sent to the slot editor, who reads it, assigns room for it in the paper and then gives it to a rim editor for copy editing, headline and cutline writing.

Late in the evening, the rim editor remembers that *Laundromat* is a brand name, like *Jell-O* and *Xerox*. A check of the stylebook suggests that the word should be changed to *coin-operated laundry*. The rim editor wonders, "Should I make the change myself? Should I leave it unchanged? Should I consult?" Would the protocol be of any help to our rim editor?

Point 6 suggests that the editor could make the change to prevent a violation of the stylebook guidelines. The editor figures that the writer did not realize the conflict and made a simple, honest mistake. The pro-tocol might permit the copy editor to make the change on her own, explaining it the next day.

But the editor also considers points 20 and 24. The first requires con-sultation for a change in a lead; the second when a change influences the tone of the story. The editor feels that while *coin-operated laundry* is tech-nically correct, it lacks the small-town feel and simplicity of *Laundromat*. At 10 p.m., she decides to consult.

But with whom?

The Poynter group drafted this statement about the standard lines of communication:

> When problems or questions arise, the rim editor should consult with the slot. If things cannot be resolved, go next to the assigning editor. The assign-ing editor consults with the reporter if necessary. If a conflict still exists, the problem should be taken to the news editor, who has the option of consulting

with the city editor. In rare cases, the managing editor would be called upon to make the final decision.

Face-to-face communication is the ideal method of solving problems; telephone conversations are next, followed by electronic messages. If assigning editors and reporters are not in the office or at home, they are required to leave numbers where they can be reached in case questions arise. On delicate stories, reporters may want to call the copy desk directly to see if they have any questions.

If a change must be made without consulting the reporter or assigning editor, the slot should explain the decision the next day, and all parties in the process should be informed about what happened.

This specific protocol does not encourage our troubled rim editor to call the reporter directly about *Laundromat* or to offer the writer a chance to make a revision that violates neither style nor the stylebook, but there is no reason why protocols should restrict rim editors from communication directly with reporters. In some cases, a formal application of the chain of command, from rim to slot to assigner to reporter, may be desirable. But any protocol that gets in the way of common sense and efficiency is not worth much.

Protocols will inevitably reflect the personality, the organizational structure and the history of the newspaper. The specifics of the document are less important than the conversational process that formulates it and that keeps it fresh and effective. That process should reflect the values of openness, collaboration and concern for the reader. Such a document has been in effect at the Charlotte Observer:

> This is a guide to help copy editors find their way through the sometimes murky issue of when to consult about changes they make in stories.
>
> This is mostly just common sense, buttressed by an assumption of professionalism, courtesy and sensitivity on all sides.
>
> To begin, some principles:
>
> **1.** Copy editors are editors, not proofreaders. They are professionals who exercise judgment, who are skilled at word-editing, who want to help the reader understand the news.
>
> **2.** Copy editors realize that it is not their names on the stories, but the reporters', so they don't edit arbitrarily. They edit to improve.
>
> **3.** Like doctors, if they cannot cure a story's ills, they will, at the very least, do no harm.
>
> **4.** When they change a story, they must be absolutely sure nothing they do changes its meaning or tone, or in any other way makes it inaccurate.

5. When in doubt, consult, if for no other reason than to help educate colleagues in good editing.

Some specifics:

A. We should always consult with the assigning editor or the reporter about:
1. "Jazzing up" a lead.
2. Editing for fairness or to remove editorializing.
3. Editing to change a story's tone.
4. Any change inside quotation marks.
5. Any change that could alter the meaning of even one sentence in the story in such a way that might make it inaccurate.

B. In many areas, whether to consult depends on the magnitude of the change or whether the change would alter meaning. Other factors that sometimes affect whether we consult: How near deadline we are, whether the story is staff-written, how sensitive the story is, how important the story is.

Here are some situations when copy editors will often want to consult with assigning editors:
1. Moving a paragraph.
2. Cutting an unnecessary paragraph.
3. Filling in a missing word.
4. Clarifying sentences.
5. Moving or adding attribution.
6. Adding background.
7. Tightening wording in a lead.
8. Trimming information from a lead.

C. Sometimes we don't need to consult with assigning editors, assuming the editing we do is appropriate, helps the story and doesn't alter the meaning or tone. These things are essential to aggressive, skilled copy editing, and we needn't ask permission to do them:
1. Correcting grammar, punctuation, usage and style errors.
2. Correcting factual errors.
3. Adding factual information, such as locaters, percentages, the correct name of an agency.
4. Cutting wordiness.
5. Clarifying language.

Explanations and feedback:

Copy editors need to be told if they make errors in copy editing. Assigning editors and reporters should know why changes are made. If a copy editor must make extensive changes in a story, or routinely makes the same change in the same reporter's story, the editor is obligated to communicate that to the reporter or assigning editor, who should talk about it with the reporter.

When a copy editor and assigning editor or reporter disagree about whether a change is needed:

1. Collaborate. Each editor should explain his or her position, and be specific.
2. Make sure the slot editor knows what the issue is. That editor can help collaborate.
3. If the impasse remains, if either editor thinks the wrong thing is going into the newspaper, consult the editor in charge of the newsroom.
4. Remember the rules of conduct: we're all trying to put out a good newspaper. We respect each other, even when we disagree. Remember the readers.

Protocols promote clarity and speed in complex news operations. More important, the collaborative process of creating and modifying a protocol promotes mutual understanding among the players. Every issue in a protocol will generate surprising exceptions, revealing underlying attitudes and values. Try creating your own, using either of the two models presented in this chapter.

SUMMARY

- No writing will improve without cooperation from copy editors.
- Copy editors save editors' and reporters' butts.
- Protocols first produce conversation and mutual understanding, and then enhance communication.
- Protocols are guidelines, not rule books.
- Copy editors are people.

WORKSHOP

1. If you have never worked on a copy desk, volunteer to work on one for a night. At least sit with a copy editor for an evening. Observe the flow of copy and the division of labor. Listen in on conversations between copy editors and assigning editors or reporters. Based on your observations, how could copy editors participate in a coaching environment?
2. Copy editors are writers too. With at least two people, conduct a headline and cutline writing exercise during which members of your group seek to help each other through consultation and coaching. See if you can come up with a list of coaching questions that are of particular use in helping someone improve a headline.

3. Observe a newsroom, looking closely at the physical location of the copy desks. Draw a little schematic in which you show the copy desks in relation to the assigning desks and reporters' desks. Ask someone at the paper to explain to you the relationship of these desks. Based on your observation and interviews, does the location of the desks contribute to consultation and collaboration, or inhibit them?

4. Some people argue that the best kind of communication is face to face, followed by communication over the telephone, by electronic mail and by exchange of memos. Discuss this premise. Interview some copy editors on which forms of communication they use most frequently. What are the special demands of each form? What role does technology play in newsroom communication?

5. This chapter discusses at length the idea of an editing protocol. Reread that discussion and form three groups to develop your own protocol, one group for each category. Don't try to match the one in the book. Start from scratch and deal with the issues that seem most important to you. Try to make sure that a variety of newsroom perspectives (reporter, assigning editor, copy editor) are represented. Share your protocol with the other groups. Discuss their similarities and differences.

6. Make believe you are starting a new newspaper. One of your goals is to achieve high morale among copy editors, without doing damage to writers and assigning editors. Write up a one-page job description for a copy editor that would attract talented people to your paper.

CHAPTER 18

Tough Questions About Coaching

Question: From what you see and hear at newspapers, do you think there's enough coaching going on?

Answer: No. Writers at most papers complain that they get *no* feedback or that the editing is too directive or too negative. Writers and editors are clearly not conversing at the front end of the process, so we get a lot of second-guessing near deadline when not much can be done to help the story. The lack of coaching also encourages too much conventional thinking: predictable story ideas and tired approaches to telling the news.

Q: Is there any kind of writer or person who can't be coached?

A: Probably yes, but only the most arrogant and obstinate. Most people want praise, and most want to develop their skills and confidence in a supportive environment, which is what coaching is all about.

Editors should always assume that any person can change. That assumption will make the editor a better journalist and a better person, even if a particular writer resists help.

Q: Don't you need highly specialized skills to be a good coach? I'm not sure I have those skills. If I don't think I know enough to coach, wouldn't it be dangerous to try?

A: Some coaching skills are very specialized. Some editors, for example, can diagnose problems more effectively than others or see the unrealized potential in a piece. But much coaching involves asking good questions and listening to the writer, and in many conferences, the writer is doing most of the talking. So, the basic coaching skills are actually reporting skills: asking good questions, respecting the writer and listening.

A Florida high school student named Krystal Heinzen once proclaimed that the most helpful writing coach she ever had was her dog CeSar. When she had a problem in a story, Krystal would call in her dog, tell CeSar to sit, and then proceed to tell the dog about the problems in the story. He would look attentive and apparently listen. Krystal would *hear herself* solve the problem. All she needed was a chance to talk about the story. So if Krystal's dog can help a writer. . . .

Q: You talk as if all editors would make good coaches. But I'd be happier if my editor would *stop* trying to coach and leave me alone. Every time my editor intervenes, the story gets worse. What should I do?

A: An editor, like a writer, may be stronger in some areas than in others. An editor with excellent news judgment may not have very well-developed language or people skills. The good organizer may not make a great coach. Top management needs to create jobs that allow people to take advantage of their strengths. An editor who lacks confidence may want to delegate coaching responsibility to another. The editor who does not coach can still help create an environment for coaching.

That answer won't help much if you're stuck with a negative, clumsy or insensitive editor. So you have one of four choices: 1) quit and find a paper where all the editors are perfect; 2) find a way to move to another department, where the editing is better; 3) suffer in silence and hope your editor dies or quits; 4) learn how to "manage up," that is, to change the behavior of a boss who's hurting your career.

Q: You talk about positive editing, but doesn't most editing have to be negative? After all, our job is to eliminate problems in stories. Isn't that an essentially negative act?

A: Let's take the case of an editor dissatisfied with a writer. The writer is not productive enough, and the stories he hands in are conventional, average quality at best.

One day the writer, having missed a couple of tentative deadlines, hands in a story. The editor reads it, and to her surprise, it is better than anything he has done so far. It reads well and even takes an unusual angle.

But the editor is blinded by her anger at this writer's persistent delays and yells at him for getting the story in late, "Why couldn't you have had this in two days ago?"

Such negative managing wastes an opportunity for improvement. The editor could say, "Now this is the kind of story I've been looking for from you. I knew you could do it. Now let's work on getting you into the paper more often. And on time."

Q: I'm a pretty lowly editor, way down on the totem pole. Don't you need special status or authority to coach?

A: No. Just do it. If you don't feel like a coach, don't worry about it. Just begin to act as you think a coaching editor would act.

Try an experiment. Put this book down and walk over to the nearest writer. Sincerely praise that reporter for something. Go ahead, do it now. We're not kidding, go do it.

Now, wasn't that amazing? Did you see that look on the writer's face? Don't you think the next story you see from that reporter will be better?

Q: Time, time, time. I don't feel I have an extra second to breathe. How can I spend time coaching when I barely have time to get the section out, much less eat lunch?

A: We worry about newsrooms where people don't have time for lunch. That usually means a misallocation of resources, or managers who don't care about burning out a staff. And it may be that your inability to coach is making your time crunch worse. So experiment with time. Test out whether one minute of early consultation can save two minutes on deadline. That same minute may save you 10 minutes of editing.

Multiply the number of reporters you have by two minutes of coaching each. Now multiply that number of reporters by 10 minutes of editing each. Subtract the coaching total from the editing total. See, coaching creates time. Every day.

Q: Isn't coaching more appropriate for long features than for spot news?

A: It is true that editors recognize the need to pay attention to important stories, so writers who work on special features or long projects are more likely to get coached. But coaching should work across the board, for all writers and all kinds of stories. It's time for editors to give some of their creative energy to coaching new kinds of short stories. If we're not writing spot news well, we're failing in one of our most important responsibilities. We also need to coach headlines and cutlines and summaries and digest items.

Q: When my editor coaches me on a special project, things go great until the "higher-ups" get their hands on it. The managing editor feels the need to change it, and then the executive editor, and then the editor, and in some cases, the publisher. The piece comes out homogenized, as if it were written by a committee. How do I prevent that?

A: Attempting to reconceive stories late in the process seldom succeeds. On the contrary, we need to challenge the concept of the story early on, when the reporter can use the feedback and advice.

If the "higher-ups" are second-guessing the "lower-downs," you might try to get the top people involved earlier in conversations about the stories. There is some danger in that, to be sure, for they have power and authority and can bend the stories if they choose. But isn't it better to have them "first-guess" the story rather than second-guess it? Give them some say early in the process in the hope that they will become shepherds for the writer's work rather than wolves ready to devour it.

Q: How do you deal with a committee of editors when each one has a different idea of how a story should be approached?

A: Get everyone in the same room to talk about the story together in a single sitting. This gathering will eliminate the assembly-line approach in which each editor unscrews one bolt at a time. You may not have to perform frustrating and time-consuming damage-control efforts.

If editors offer conflicting advice, consider yourself lucky that you are getting any response in advance of publication. Then pick and choose among the pieces of advice.

Q: My editor sometimes pretends to coach by telling me to rewrite a line instead of doing it himself. It amounts to the same thing: he gets his way, and the story gets rewritten in his words eventually. What to do?

A: Your editor may not understand the difference between coaching and fixing, so talk to him about it, if you're brave enough. Also ask him to articulate why he prefers his sentence over yours. Maybe he'll say: "Because it is in the active voice" or "Because it begins with the subject and the verb." There may be some sound coaching advice behind what seems like purely subjective responses. He might also hear himself saying something like "Because I want it that way." Just sit there and let his words sink in.

Q: I often disagree about changes my editor wants to make in my story. What do I do if that happens?

A: Coaching can be a tough business. Story conferences will often inspire heated discussion and debate, resulting in negotiation and compromise. If an editor and reporter disagree about a change, one of them may want to suggest a third alternative. If neither A nor B satisfies them both, perhaps C will do the trick. In some cases, a third party can come in to consult, what some people call "a fresh eye."

Q: Isn't it true that only weak or inexperienced writers benefit from coaching?

A: All writers need coaching. Editors normally ignore some writers who produce acceptable work, and pay attention to the "problem cases." But coaching should not be a punishment for unsatisfactory work; it should be a reward for continuing effort. Important opportunities are lost when editors can't find the time to take a B story and help turn it into an A. Good writers who don't get any editing can turn into prima donnas who don't want any.

In the best newspapers, the best writers sign up first to confer with visiting coaches. They think they need the most help, and they try out the techniques the coach suggests.

Q: How do you find time for coaching on a staff that's lean and mean to the point of starvation?

A: A starving staff has got to be fed before malnutrition does them all in. Coaching is the food that builds staff morale. The less staff you think you have, the more you need to develop a coaching environment. The less time you think you have, the more time you need to create for coaching.

Very often, the lean and mean staff becomes a collaborative team that produces exceptional work.

Q: The newspaper is okay the way it is. Shouldn't we just leave things alone?

A: Good coaching helps preserve the best traditions of good work at a paper. But it also helps inspire creativity and innovation. If you don't want those things, fine, don't coach. But get ready for the competition to pass you by. Stand still and die.

Q: Why should only writers get coaching? What about the rest of us?

A: Line editors, copy editors, photographers, artists and managers all benefit from coaching. A newspaper that focuses only on the work of writers misses an important opportunity to develop the whole staff. Coaching gets writers, for example, to think about collaboration with photographers, page designers and artists who produce informational graphics. The resulting marriage of writing, editing and design serves the reader.

Q: Editing is often very subjective, so coaching must be too. What if I tell a reporter one thing, and another editor tells the reporter something completely different?

A: *Vive la différence!* A thousand readers respond to the clearest article in a thousand different ways. The writer does not write for *the* reader but for readers. A variety of early responses gives the writer new choices.

Q: Why should we bother coaching, when any good we do is always zapped on the copy desk?

A: You've probably made the mistake of leaving the copy editors out of the coaching process. Too often, reporters ignore these important players or treat them as second-class journalists. As fellow professionals, they benefit from programs that help them grow. Begin healing the wounds by establishing a "protocol," as described in Chapter 17, Copy Editors as Partners.

Q: Is there really a place in daily journalism for this touchy-feely coaching stuff? I'm an editor, not a nursemaid or a babysitter. Professionals don't need to have their hands held, do they?

A: Your question reflects an old macho tradition in American journalism, glamorized by dozens of old movies, like "Teacher's Pet," in which a city editor played by Clark Gable teaches writing to young reporters by chewing them out and throwing things. But at least he was coaching, not in the most enlightened style, to be sure, but he, and the generation of editors he represented, took their tutoring roles seriously.

"I expected to come to this paper and learn how to write," said one young reporter at a large daily. "But I've been here two years, and I haven't learned a thing about writing."

That reporter doesn't need to have his hand held. He needs someone willing to help him so he will stay in the business and at his newspaper rather than flee in disillusionment to public relations or law school.

Q: Do women make better coaches than men?

A: No better, no worse. A diverse newsroom, where many people coach, provides a variety of responses for the writer. The popular stereotype tells us that women are more supportive and nurturing than men, so one might think that they would make excellent coaches. At one North Carolina paper, the reporters refer to their city editor affectionately as "Ma News."

Unfortunately, the most supportive journalists do not necessarily become editors. Too often, papers promote the most aggressive and ambitious staffers rather than those with people skills. And women and minority editors often believe they should emulate the behavior of the most obnoxious editors rather than the most supportive. Such traps undercut the potential of a truly diverse newsroom.

Q: List six things that would improve the quality of coaching at a newspaper.

A: 1. Pay attention to coaching as a criterion for hiring and promotion.
   2. Develop apprenticeships for writers who want to become coaching editors.
   3. Teach coaching in your newsroom, through workshops, brown-bag lunches, reading and daily conversation.
   4. Ask writers what they need to do their best work.
   5. Talk to each other in the newsroom.
   6. Buy your editor this book!

CHAPTER 19

The Courage to Coach

If you've read this far in this book, you probably believe that coaching will work for you. You want to try it, but don't know how to start.

Here's how: *just do it.*

Starting to coach needs no consultation with higher authorities, no fanfare, no announcements. Just start by coaching one of your writers, preferably a strong writer with whom you already have a good relationship. Your best and most enthusiastic and most willing reporters will help you get the hang of it. With top writers, you can usually see the results of coaching right away, and they will exult in new confidence in front of everybody.

Wait awhile before tackling very weak writers. Getting them up to snuff may take months or years. And the problems of some poor writers lie too deep for coaches anyway. So, gain some experience and confidence before you take on the toughest challenges.

Process coaching will get a coaching program off the ground in a hurry. Start brainstorming on assignments to get the reporters' minds and eyes open, with questions like these:

"What's the County Commission up to today, Jane?"
"Who are the major players?"
"Expect any surprises?"
"Any documents available?"
"Great. Touch base when you get back."

Keep it short and simple.

Next, debrief reporters when they come back to the office. Ask 90 seconds worth of short and easy questions like these:

"What've you got, Jay?"
"What's the story about?"
"What's the lead about?"
"How long should it be?"
"When can I have it?"
"Great. Go to it."

Keep it short and simple.

Lurk in the newsroom so reporters can see you're available for consultation. If they don't come to you, go to them with questions like this:

"How's it going, Myrtle?"
"Need any help, Jack?"
"Liked your piece yesterday, Joan. Give me another one that good."

Half the battle in coaching is just getting out among the reporters.

Now for the hard part. Coaching goes against our tradition of hostile and distant editors, and writers will react with surprise to anyone who starts acting like a friendly collaborator. They may think you've lost your mind. Let them. Sooner or later, someone will ask what's going on. Just tell them. Ask for their help. Word will spread.

Some people in the newsroom will regard coaching as soft, as somehow likely to undermine the control of editors. Coaching is just a different way of getting our essential work done. When other people see how it works better than the old ways, the criticism will cease.

One final problem: old habits die hard. In our haste to get the paper out, we lapse into the old diet of screaming, taking control of other people's stories, relying on red pens, and sniping about stylebook issues. Recognize it when you see yourself doing it, and stop it.

Coaching is not a magic pill to solve all the problems of the workplace. But it's more than just another tool in our kit. It's a means of creating a humane newsroom.

Some of you are reading this book to find a new way to do a better job. Perhaps the old way has you feeling worn out, burned out or battered down. Maybe you're tired of fighting with writers or bosses. Maybe you're demoralized by the endless cycle of daily battles and are considering leaving the profession. Or maybe you're the brand-new city editor and don't want to repeat the mistakes of your predecessors.

The most important requirement for creating change is courage. You may not feel like a coach, but don't let that stop you. Make believe you're one. Act the way you think a coaching editor should act, one writer and one story at a time. As you change your behavior, new attitudes and values will follow. People, especially eager writers, will support you in your work and look to you for guidance. Your career, perhaps your life, will change. And it will all be because you ask good questions. And listen.

A Coaching Exercise

Many journalists remain skeptical of coaching, mostly because it seems slow and apparently requires great analytical skills. Editors think they don't have time to learn coaching, much less practice it.

Coaching skills are essentially reporting skills: asking good questions and listening to the answers. In our opinion, almost anyone can learn to coach with proper guidance. At the Poynter Institute, we routinely teach a roomful of journalists to coach in an exercise that lasts about two hours.

We adopted and modified this exercise from one conducted at the institute by Donald Murray. This drill gives people the experience of coaching and being coached, and they succeed almost without instruction. We will describe our version here, but you can modify it for your own purposes and situations. We change our procedure almost seminar by seminar.

Write the following plan on the board:

1. Write down two topics	two minutes
2. Coach on choosing one topic	two minutes times three
3. Choose topic and plan	two minutes
4. Coach on plan for piece	two minutes times three
5. Write the top	five minutes
6. Coach on writing rest of piece	four minutes times three

Divide the group into threes. Provide each group with paper to write on. A few index cards or a yellow pad will do.

Tell the group that the exercise will give them three experiences: coaching, getting coached and watching coaching. Tell them they need to know only three things to proceed:

1. Let the writer talk first.
2. Listen to what the writer says.
3. Help the writer, not the copy.

Explain the entire exercise, and repeat the instructions for each part as you go along. Assure them that no one will ask them to read their pieces aloud to the *whole* group. Invite them to relax and enjoy themselves.

Step 1. Jotting Down Topics

Give the following instructions: "For stage one, all of you are writers. In the next two minutes, jot down two ideas on a card. You might want to write a column on a personal topic, something you can write on the spot." Then time two minutes and signal a halt somehow. Perhaps ring a bell, which irritates people but gets their attention.

Step 2. Coaching on Topic Choice

Say: "In this stage, we will coach each other to help the writer pick one topic to write on. We'll divide up each group into three players: writer, coach and observer." Then explain some scheme to determine the roles.

Now say: "In two minutes, the writer will describe the two topics, and the coach will ask friendly questions to help the writer select one topic to write on. Obviously, the writer has to talk fast so the coach has time to ask questions. The observer will simply observe and may not speak. We're going to do this three times, with each person playing each role. Everybody understand? Do you know what role you're playing for this first round? Good. Two minutes, go."

After two minutes, signal a halt. Tell everyone that the roles will shift one position, with the coach becoming the writer, the observer becoming the coach, and the writer the observer. Say: "Now do you see why the writer has to talk fast? Understand who you are this round? Good, two minutes, go."

After two minutes, shift again and finish step 2.

Step 3. Planning the Piece

Say: "In this step, everyone is a writer. Choose just one of your topics to write on and organize your materials, essentially designing a structure for the whole piece. You can write a plan, an outline, a diagram, a paragraph, anything that will explain your proposed structure to your group. Any questions? You have two minutes. Go."

Time two minutes and conclude step 3.

Step 4. Coaching the Plan

Say: "In this step, the writer will explain the proposed structure, and the coach will help improve that structure. The observer will listen but not speak. We'll use the same initial roles and sequence as before, and we'll do it three times so that everyone plays all three roles. Everybody understand? Do you know which role you will play first? Good, go."

Time two minutes. Repeat the step twice more until everyone has played writer, coach, and observer.

Step 5. Writing the Top

Now say: "In this step, each of you becomes a writer again. In the next five minutes, write the top of the personal column, just a lead or a few graphs. Don't write a lot because you will have very little time to read it aloud to your group. [Point to the speed demon of the group.] X, of course, will probably write the whole thing in four minutes. Everybody clear? Five minutes, go."

Time five minutes, and conclude step 5.

Step 6. Coaching the Whole Piece

Say: "In this final step, the writer will read the top of the piece to the small group *quickly*, and the coach will then help the writer think about the rest of the column. The observer will not speak, please. Remember, focus on the writer, not the copy. We'll do this three times, so everyone gets a chance to play all three roles. Writers, you have to read fast to allow time for coaching and discussion. Everybody clear? Four minutes, go."

Repeat twice so everyone plays writer, coach and observer. Give them a few moments to unwind before starting a discussion.

Debriefing the Exercise

In this phase, use coaching techniques to let the group discover what they have experienced and learned. Help them to realize that coaching is quick, easy, helpful and fun. Lead a discussion by asking a series of questions, not in any particular order after the first few:

1. Raise your hand, who feels that coaching helped improve what you just wrote?
2. Raise your hand, who feels their coach did a good job?
3. Did you feel you had enough time to coach and be coached?
4. Which techniques worked? (Listening, smiling, asking personal questions, and so on).
5. Which techniques did not work? (Correcting copy, powerplays, not listening, arguing, and so on).
6. What was your experience as an observer?
7. Evaluate your own performance as a coach.
8. And so on, developing the idea that coaching is simple and easy to do.

Toward the end, remind the group how much time they spent writing: two minutes jotting topics, two minutes choosing and organizing, and five minutes drafting, for a total of nine. Help them to see that very few stories get that far along in nine minutes.

Then remind the group how long each person spent coaching: two minutes on the topics, two minutes on the structure, and four minutes on the rest of the piece, for a total of eight minutes. Remind them how much instruction they received: three sentences. Then remind them how almost everyone thought their coach performed well. Coaching is easy to do with the most basic reporter skills: asking good questions and listening.

Give out a handout at this point, and discuss some of the finer points of coaching technique. If you give out the handout earlier, people will simply paraphrase it in discussion.

Your Version

This exercise has worked well with professional journalists, students and journalism professors in a variety of settings. You can tailor this exercise to your own situation. You might want to give more time for writing and planning, or add a step for lead writing. To save time, you might delete steps 1 and 2, and go directly to coaching on structure.

Finally, this exercise has one unexpected side effect: many participants say they have never written a personal column before and now want to try a real one. The exercise gives them permission to write about themselves. Coaching frees writers.

BIBLIOGRAPHY

A Reading List for Coaches

This list contains all works mentioned in the text, along with other suggested reading that will advance your understanding of coaching, reporting and editing, and the character and behavior of writers.

Berg, A. Scott. *Max Perkins: Editor of Genius.* New York: Dutton, 1978. A reverential biography of America's most famous book editor.

Best Newspaper Writing. Karen Brown, Roy Peter Clark and Don Fry, eds. St. Petersburg, Fla.: The Poynter Institute for Media Studies. Published annually since 1979. Reprints the winning stories from the American Society of Newspaper Editors Distinguished Writing awards, plus interviews with the writers. Includes annual bibliography on writing, editing and coaching.

Blundell, William E. *The Art and Craft of Feature Writing: Based on the Wall Street Journal.* New York: New American Library, 1988. Blundell is the genius on story organization.

Brande, Dorothea. *Becoming a Writer.* Los Angeles: J. P. Tarcher, 1981. Reprint of 1934 edition published by Harcourt Brace. This rediscovered classic reveals the complex personalities of writers.

Calkins, Lucy McCormick. *The Art of Teaching Writing.* Portsmouth, N.H.: Heinemann Educational Books, 1986. An experienced teacher conducts writing conferences with children.

Clark, Roy Peter. *Free to Write: A Journalist Teaches Young Writers.* Portsmouth, N.H.: Heinemann Educational Books, 1987. Bridges the gap between the classroom and coaching in the newsroom.

The Coaches' Corner. A Quarterly Exchange on Coaching Writers. Paul Salsini, Milwaukee Journal, Box 661, Milwaukee, WI 53201, and Lucille deView, Orange County Register, Santa Ana, CA 92701, eds. Articles from the most thoughtful writing coaches in America.

Faber, John. *Great News Photos and the Stories Behind Them.* 2nd ed. New York: Dover Publications, 1978. (See pp. 102–03.) Photographer Nat Fein heeds his editor's advice and wins a Pulitzer Prize.

Franklin, Jon. *Writing for Story.* New York: Atheneum, 1986. The author offers a system for organizing powerful non-fiction.

Goldberg, Natalie. *Wild Mind: Living the Writer's Life.* New York: Bantam Books, 1990. A quirky look at freeing up writers.

177

Graves, Donald H. *Writing: Teachers and Children at Work.* Portsmouth, N.H.: Heinemann Educational Books, 1983. Working with very young children, the author shows how to *receive* the work of writers.

Lanson, Gerald, and Mitchell Stephens. "Jell-O Journalism: Why Reporters Have Gone Soft in Their Leads." *Washington Journalism Review* (April 1982), pp. 21–23. A provocative attack on self-indulgent journalism.

Mencher, Melvin. *News Reporting and Writing.* 4th ed. Dubuque, Iowa: Wm. C. Brown Publishers, 1987. The best-written textbook on the reporting craft.

Murray, Donald M. "The Listening Eye: Reflections on the Writing Conference." *Learning by Teaching: Selected Articles on Writing and Teaching.* Montclair, N.J.: Boynton/Cook, 1982. An essay on how to confer with college writers.

—————. *Shoptalk: Learning to Write with Writers.* Portsmouth, N.H.: Boynton/Cook, 1990. Hundreds of pungent quotations from writers on the craft of writing.

—————. *Writing for Your Readers.* Chester, Ct.: Globe Pequot Press, 1983. Great advice on the writing process, from a veteran coach working at the Boston Globe.

Scanlan, Christopher, ed. *How I Wrote the Story.* Providence, R.I.: The Providence Journal Company, 1986. Scanlan, along with Joel Rawson and Donald Murray, shows how to build relationships between writers and editors.

Stepp, Carl Sessions. *Editing for Today's Newsroom: New Perspectives for a Changing Profession.* Hillsdale, N.J.: Lawrence Erlbaum Associates, 1989. One of the only editing texts available that offers helpful advice on the human side of editing.

Strunk, William, Jr., and E. B. White. *Elements of Style.* 3rd ed. New York: Macmillan, 1979. The bible for writers and editors.

Wheelock, John Hall, ed. *Editor to Author: The Letters of Maxwell E. Perkins.* New York: Charles Scribner's Sons, 1987. A great editor corresponds with his writers.

Zinsser, William. "Write as Well as You Can." *On Writing Well.* 3rd ed. New York: Harper & Row, 1985. Advice for writers on how to work effectively with editors.

INDEX